EFFECTIVE EXECUTIVE'S

The Seven Core Skills Required to Turn Windows 2000 Professional into a Business Power Tool

GUIDE TO WINDOWS 2000

EFFECTIVE EXECUTIVE'S

**The Seven Core Skills Required to Turn Windows 2000
Professional into a Business Power Tool**

GUIDE TO WINDOWS 2000

Pat Coleman

**REDMOND
TECHNOLOGY
PRESS**

Effective Executive's Guide to Windows 2000:
The Seven Core Skills Required to Turn Windows 2000 Professional into a Business Power Tool

Published by
Redmond Technology Press
8581 154ᵗʰ Avenue NE
Redmond, WA 98052
www.redtechpress.com

Library of Congress Catalog Card No: applied for

ISBN 0-9672981-8-0

Printed and bound in the United States of America.

9 8 7 6 5 4 3 2 1

Distributed by
Independent Publishers Group
814 N. Franklin St.
Chicago, IL 60610
www.ipgbook.com

Contents at a Glance

Contents

Skill 2	**Manage Files and Folders**	**31**

Skill 3   **Print with Windows 2000 Professional   63**

Skill 4   ## Work on a Network   **89**

Skill 5   **Customize Windows 2000 Professional**   **127**

INTRODUCTION

The *Effective Executive's* series is written specifically for the business professional. The purpose is to provide you with the information you need to use your computer effectively to get your job done. Unless you are an information technology specialist, your job is not to know everything about your computer. Your job is to manage sales representatives, plan a marketing campaign, design new products for your industry, manage the assets of your corporation, consult with clients, and so on. The computer is a tool for helping you to complete any of these tasks more efficiently and faster and serves as a communications medium within and outside your organization.

Therefore, the books in the *Effective Executive's* series are short (or nonexistent) on theory and quick and to the point in terms of the topic software. They focus on the precise steps or skills you need in order to use the software in your office, whether it's at a large corporation, a business you run from home, or somewhere in between.

The purpose of this book, then, is to help you acquire the skills you need as you get started with, use, and continue to learn about Microsoft Windows 2000 Professional so that it enhances your ability to do your job.

What Is Windows 2000?

An *operating system* is the set of programs responsible for the basic operation of a computer. Without an operating system, you can't run a word processor, a spreadsheet program, or a device, such as a printer or a modem. The operating system establishes rules that applications must follow in order to function correctly; for example, how many characters a filename can have and the procedure for saving and opening files.

Windows 2000 is a family of four operating systems:

- Windows 2000 Professional

- Windows 2000 Server

- Windows 2000 Advanced Server

- Windows 2000 Data Center Server

Each operating system serves a specific purpose and is appropriate for use in particular situations.

You can run *Windows 2000 Professional,* which looks much like Windows 98 and Windows Me, on a standalone computer, on a small network, or on a large network. It can act as a client or as a server, as you will see in this book.

Windows 2000 Server is an operating system that runs on a network server machine. You can run Windows 2000 Server on anything from a small network to a network of thousands of users.

Windows 2000 Advanced Server is an operating system for use by enterprises that work with large database applications and online transaction processing. For example, airline reservations systems, banks, and oil companies would use Windows 2000 Advanced Server.

Windows 2000 Data Center Server is for large-scale Internet and intranet operations.

This book focuses on Windows 2000 Professional, which you might be using in a variety of situations:

- On your desktop connected to a corporate network that uses Windows 2000 Server

- On your desktop connected to a corporate network that uses Windows NT 4 Server, the predecessor to Windows 2000

- On a small network that includes Windows 2000 Professional, Windows 98, and Windows 95 machines or only Windows 2000 Professional machines

- On a standalone computer

Regardless of the situation, Windows 2000 Professional is in use because it is a more reliable and a more secure operating system than any previous versions of Windows. If you've used previous versions of Windows, the skills you acquired apply directly and immediately to using Windows 2000 Professional. You'll see quickly, though, that you'll need additional skills to function at top speed in this new environment.

What This Book Assumes About You

First, this book assumes that you are not new to computers or new to the Windows world. It also assumes that you know how to use a mouse and a keyboard and that you know how to find and use windows and dialog boxes. It further assumes that you are an intelligent, capable business user who wants to get the most from Windows 2000 Professional while maintaining a busy schedule, achieving professional goals, and having a life.

How This Book Is Organized

Given these assumptions, this book walks you through the steps to acquire seven practical skills.

Skill 1: Understand the Desktop

The desktop is what you see when you first log on to Windows 2000 Professional. This skill explains logging on, using the Start menu, using the taskbar, working with the desktop icons, and creating shortcuts.

Skill 2: Manage Files and Folders

How you organize the information on your computer determines to a large extent how quickly you can find and use that information. This skill explains the Windows 2000 Professional file systems, how to organize documents using Windows Explorer, how to set permissions on files and folders, how to work with offline files, how to use folder options, and how to back up and restore files and folders (the best insurance you can have against computer disasters).

Skill 3: Print with Windows 2000 Professional

No matter how wired your office and how much you might want to embrace the age of electronics, you still have to print from time to time. This skill shows you how to install and manage a local printer, how to print documents, how to customize the printing process, and how to install and use fonts.

Skill 4: Work on a Network

Even if you aren't working on a network now and don't have any plans for setting one up in your business, don't skip this skill. It gives you step-by-step instructions for setting up a small network, installing a network printer, setting up users and groups, and installing network applications. In addition, it gives you information about connecting to a corporate network in a variety of ways.

Skill 5: Customize Windows 2000 Professional

Although Windows 2000 Professional will work fine just as it comes out of the box, you can personalize it in myriad ways. For example, if you have a visual or mobility impairment, you can set up the screen, the mouse, and the keyboard so that they are more accessible for you. This skill also includes a number of other suggestions for ways to customize everything from the display to the hardware.

Skill 6: Use the Internet

Depending on the nature of your business, you might easily spend the longest length of time using the Internet features of Windows 2000 Professional, which include Internet Explorer (the Web browser) and Outlook Express (the application you use to send and receive e-mail). This skill tells you how to connect to the Internet and how to use Internet Explorer and Outlook Express. In addition, it gives you some suggestions for managing your electronic office.

Skill 7: Perform Preventive Maintenance and Troubleshooting

Although Windows 2000 Professional has been touted as an extremely secure and reliable operating system, the time will come when you'll need to recover from a disaster to repair some part of the system. This skill gives you guidelines for protecting the health of your computer, maintaining the system, and troubleshooting when a problem arises.

NOTE *In addition to the seven skills, or chapters, described in the preceding paragraphs, the* Effective Executive's Guide to Windows 2000 *also includes two appendixes and a glossary of Windows 2000 Professional and Internet terms. Appendix A, "Reviewing the Windows 2000 Professional Accessories," discusses Address Book, NetMeeting, Notepad, WordPad, Fax Service, and Calculator. Appendix B, "Using Windows 2000 Professional on a Portable Computer," discusses how to dock and undock a portable, how to conserve battery life, and how to connect remotely when you're on the road.*

Conventions Used in This Book

To identify screen elements, the first letter of each word in the description is capitalized. Although this convention might look a bit strange at first, it makes it easier to understand some instructions, such as "Click the Prompt For Password When Computer Goes Off Standby check box."

You'll also find Notes, Tips, and Warnings, which point out tidbits of useful information. Pay attention to Warnings; they help you avoid potential problems.

Skill 1

UNDERSTAND THE DESKTOP

Featuring:

- Logging On
- Using the Start Menu
- Using the Taskbar
- Using the Desktop Icons
- Creating Shortcuts
- Tips for Users of Previous Versions of Windows

If you pay any attention to the computer press—or to the popular press, for that matter—you might be tempted to conclude that Windows 2000 Professional is an end in itself. That, of course, is nonsense. The most important thing about any software is that it helps get the work done easier, better, or faster or all three. Windows 2000 Professional can certainly help you and the people you work with to do your jobs easier, better, and faster, and also provide a great deal of comfort about how safe the information on your computer is—although that is the case only if you know how to use the program.

This skill introduces you to the *desktop,* what you see after you first log on to your Windows 2000 Professional system. Theoretically, the Windows desktop is analogous to your physical desktop. Opinions vary about how far this analogy extends without breaking down, and some technology experts refer to the desktop as a *shell,* a term that normally refers to the user's environment as opposed to what's really going on inside a system that makes it work.

Nonetheless, this book calls the desktop the desktop, and this skill describes all its part and pieces, tells you what each was designed to do, and shows you how to use it. If you've used other versions of Windows—Windows NT Workstation, Windows 98, or Windows 95—much of this information will look familiar, although you have a few surprises in store. Some features have new names, some features have new homes on the desktop, and some features are new.

Before getting started, though, here's one important reminder: The primary difference between Windows 2000 Professional and Windows Me, Windows 98, or Windows 95 is security. In Windows 2000 Professional, you can't do anything unless you have permission to do so. Broadly speaking, the Windows 2000 Professional universe is divided into administrators and users. Simply put, if you want to make a configuration change to your system—for example, installing new software—you must be logged on as an administrator. If you are working on a corporate network, you most likely do not have administrator privileges, although there is a system administrator who does. If you are running your own small network at home or in a small organization, you may have administrator privileges because you set yourself up as an administrator when you installed Windows 2000 Professional. Keep these security features in mind as this skill explores the desktop.

Logging On

If you've used Windows 98 or Windows 95, you might be accustomed to seeing a Log On dialog box whenever you start your computer. You also might be accustomed to simply pressing Escape or Enter to bypass this seeming inconvenience. You can't do this in Windows 2000 Professional. If you don't have a valid username and password and enter them correctly, you can't do anything on a Windows 2000 Professional system. And if you are connected to a corporate network (local area network), you might also need the name of a domain if you're supposed to log on to a domain other than the default.

NOTE   *A domain can be the description of a single computer, a department, or a complete network and is used for administrative and naming purposes.*

To log on, in the Log On To Windows dialog box, enter your username and your password. As an added security measure, a system administrator might also require you to press Ctrl+Alt+Del to display the Log On To Windows dialog box.

In Windows 2000 Professional, a username can be a maximum of 20 characters and is not case sensitive. A password can be a maximum of 127 characters and *is* case sensitive. If you are on a mixed network, for example, in which you have both Windows 2000 Professional and Windows 98 or Windows 95 machines, keep the password to a maximum of 14 characters, which is the maximum that Windows 98 or Windows 95 will recognize.

If you are on a corporate LAN, your system administrator will probably initially assign your username and your password, and you can then change your password to some favorite expression. Most corporate system administrators set your password to expire after 30 days, and they set the password history so that you can't reuse a password until you've used 12 or 13 other passwords.

Passwords are an important part of the security of a network system. The following list presents some guidelines that lead to the creation of strong passwords and, therefore, make it difficult for someone to break into your system using the usual cracking tools:

- Never use as your password any term available in a dictionary.

- Your password should be at least seven characters long and contain letters, numbers, and symbols.

- Your password should not contain your name or your username. Product names, business names, children's names, pets names, or any names or expressions that people associate with you also do not make a strong password.

- Do not continue to use the same password for long periods, even if you can.

TIP   *If your password isn't accepted, check the Caps Lock key. Remember that your password is case sensitive. If you originally entered it using all lowercase or a combination of upper- and lowercase characters and the Caps Lock key is on, your password obviously won't be accepted.*

Using the Start Menu

You can get started using the desktop by clicking icons or by using the Start menu. This skill first looks at using the Start menu and then looks at the desktop icons in a later section. The Start button is located on the far left end of the taskbar (discussed shortly); you click the button to open a menu from which you can navigate to various resources on your system. Before you click the Start button, though, your desktop looks similar to the one shown in Figure 1-1.

Figure 1-1 The Windows 2000 Professional desktop.

You might have more or fewer icons on your desktop, depending on what is installed on your system. Except for the FullShot99 icon, the desktop shown in Figure 1-1 is what you'll see the first time you start Windows 2000 Professional if you or your systems administrator hasn't installed additional applications. (FullShot99 is the program I used to create the illustrations in this book.)

Now click the Start button, and you'll see something similar to what's shown in Figure 1-2.

TIP   *If you don't see the Start button, move your cursor to the bottom of the screen.*

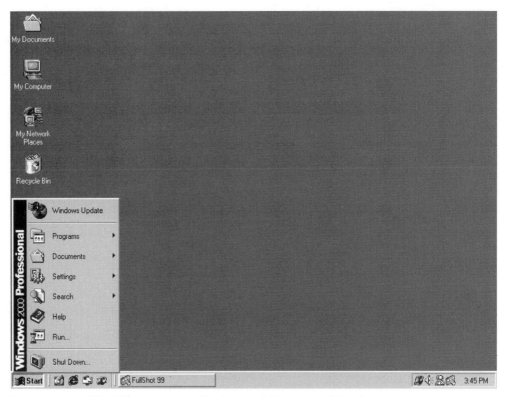

Figure 1-2   The Windows 2000 Professional desktop and the Start menu.

Connecting to the Windows Update site

Windows Update is a Microsoft site from which you can obtain product updates, technical support, and online help, among other things. When you click the Start button and then click Windows Update, a Web page similar to the one shown in Figure 1-3 opens in Internet Explorer. (Internet Explorer is discussed in detail in Skill 6.) Click the Product Updates link if you want to be notified whenever Microsoft posts a critical new update for Windows 2000 Professional.

Figure 1-3   The Microsoft Windows Update page.

Finding programs

Although you can open programs on your system in a number of ways, one of the most straightforward is to click the Start button, click Programs, and then click a program from the submenu that's displayed. At the very least, you'll see the following items on the Programs menu:

- Accessories contains yet another submenu of programs that come with Windows 2000 Professional. Read about these programs in Appendix A.

- Startup contains the names of programs you want to use every time you start Windows 2000 Professional.

- Internet Explorer is the Web browser included with Windows 2000 Professional. Internet Explorer is discussed in detail in Skill 6.

- Outlook Express is the mail and news reader that's included with Windows 2000 Professional. Outlook Express is discussed in Skill 6.

A new feature in Windows 2000 Professional is personalized menus. You know about this feature if you've used any of the applications included with the Microsoft Office 2000 suite. A *personalized* menu includes only those items you've used most recently. You can see the other items on the menu by clicking the More button (the double chevron) at the bottom of the menu. Some people find this to be a great way to simplify and streamline the Start menu, while others find it a nuisance. You can decide for yourself and then turn it off if you don't like it. To disable personalized menus, follow these steps:

1. **Open the Taskbar And Start Menu Properties dialog box.**

   Click the Start button, click Settings, and then click Taskbar & Start Menu. (You can also right-click an empty area of the taskbar and choose Properties to open this dialog box. You can read about right-clicking later in this skill.)

2. **Disable personalized menus.**

   On the General tab, click the Use Personalized Menus check box to clear it, and then click OK.

NOTE   *Later, this skill looks at how to use the taskbar.*

Finding documents

How you manage your files and folders so that you can easily find a document is a topic the next skill looks at in depth. Using the guidelines in Skill 2, you can go a long way toward always putting your cursor on the document you want. Don't forget, however, about the Documents menu on the Start menu. The menu contains a list of the last 15 documents you opened in addition to your My Documents folder. When you select a document name from this list, the document usually opens immediately in the application in which it was created.

One exception to the preceding sentence is an image file. When you select an image file from the Documents menu, it opens in Imaging Preview even though you might have created it, for example, in PhotoShop. To specify the program in which a type of document always opens, follow these steps:

1. **Display the Open With dialog box.**

   Click the Start button, click Documents, right-click the name of a document in the list, and select Choose Program from the shortcut menu.

2. **Associate a program with a document.**

   Select a program from the list in the Open With dialog box, and then click OK.

NOTE   *If you don't see the program you want on the list, click Other, select a program, and click Open. Windows 2000 Professional adds the program to the list. Select the program, and click OK.*

To clear the items on the Documents menu, follow these steps:

1. Open the Taskbar And Start Menu Properties dialog box.

Click the Start button, click Settings, and then click Taskbar & Start Menu.

2. Tell Windows 2000 Professional that you want to start a fresh Documents menu.

Click the Advanced tab, click the Clear button, and then click OK.

Clearing the Documents menu doesn't delete the documents from your system. It simply empties the list and makes room for more recent items.

Right-clicking

This skill mentioned earlier that there's more to say about right-clicking in Windows 2000 Professional, and this section does that. Before getting into right-clicking, however, you need to know a little about shortcut menus. If you've used Windows NT 4, Windows Me, Windows 98, or Windows 95, you're familiar with shortcut menus, although you might have heard them referred to as context menus or even right-click menus. The reason for the alternative terms is that you can right-click any number of items in Windows 2000 Professional to display a menu of context-sensitive commands that are appropriate for the item you clicked.

For example, if you right-click an item on the Documents menu, you'll see a shortcut menu similar to the one shown in Figure 1-4. I right-clicked on an image file to display the shortcut menu that's shown, which contains commands appropriate in that context. I can choose Print to immediately begin printing the document, choose Delete to immediately send the document to the Recycle Bin, or choose Properties to open the Properties dialog box for this document, for example.

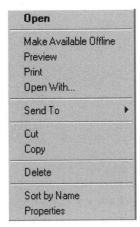

Figure 1-4   A typical shortcut menu in Windows 2000 Professional.

You can right-click almost anywhere in Windows 2000 Professional and display something useful. In some cases, you display not a shortcut menu but rather a What's This? box that you can click to get help with the item you clicked. If you're ever in doubt, just right-click. You can never hurt anything, and in the worst case can usually undo most things you might do.

If you're still not a believer in the virtues of right-clicking, consider one more example of how it can save you time and effort. Suppose that you want to open Windows Explorer, the program you use to manage your files and folders. You can do so in the following ways:

- Click the Start button, click Programs, click Accessories to open the Accessories menu, and then click Windows Explorer.

- Right-click the My Computer icon on the desktop, and click Explore.

There's no question about which technique is quicker.

NOTE   *In the next skill, you'll get a good look at how to use Windows Explorer.*

Understanding settings

In Windows 2000 Professional, you use the items on the Settings menu to open yet another item with which you can configure your computer system in some way. For example, you might want to set the date and time (and you can do so if you have permission), set the sounds associated with certain Windows functions, or enable or disable personalized menus, for example. To take care of such tasks, you click the Start button, click Settings, and then use an item on the Settings menu, which is shown in Figure 1-5.

Figure 1-5   The Settings menu.

Control Panel

When you click Control Panel, you'll see the screen shown in Figure 1-6. Control Panel consists of *applets,* or small programs you use to personalize Windows 2000 Professional. For example, if you are left-handed and want to configure your mouse so that the default buttons are reversed, you open the Mouse applet in Control Panel. Skill 5 describes in detail how you can use Control Panel to personalize your system.

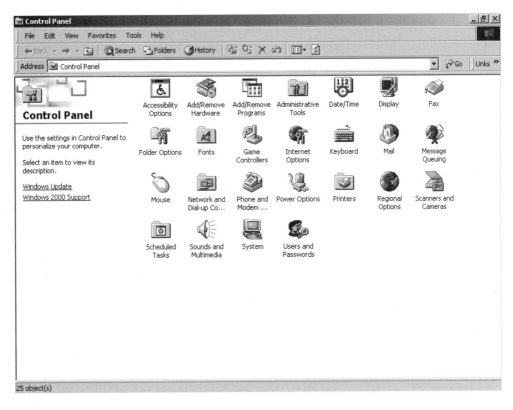

Figure 1-6   Using Control Panel applets to customize your system.

Network And Dial-Up Connections

When you click Network And Dial-Up Connections, you open the Network And Dial-Up Connections folder, which you can use to create a new network connection, check the status of a local area connection, and connect to the Internet. This folder is described in detail in Skill 4.

Printers

When you click Printers, you open the Printers folder, which you use to install a new printer and get information about the printers installed on your system. Skill 3 shows you how to use the Printers folder to install a local printer and a network printer and how to manage your printers.

Taskbar & Start Menu

When you click Taskbar & Start Menu, you open the Taskbar And Start Menu Properties dialog box, which is shown in the following section, in Figure 1-13. As mentioned earlier, you can also right-click the taskbar and choose Properties from the shortcut menu to open this dialog box. Skill 5 discusses how you can use this dialog box to personalize your system.

Searching and finding

Suppose that your to-do list frequently contains more tasks than you can cross off in a day or you want to avoid spending time looking for an important document. The next skill shows you how to manage your computer's files and folders so that you can almost always put your finger on exactly what you need. Even in the best of all possible organizational schemes, however, we all occasionally misplace something or just plain forget where we filed it. The Search command on the Start menu can be your best friend on these occasions.

When you click Search, you'll see a submenu you can use to find files and folders, a person, or a Web site. You'll probably most often use Search to locate a file or a folder, and the next skill goes into detail about how to do this task. For now, follow these steps for a preview of how Search works:

1. **Open the Search Results dialog box, which is shown in Figure 1-7.**

    Click the Start button, click Search, and then click For Files Or Folders.

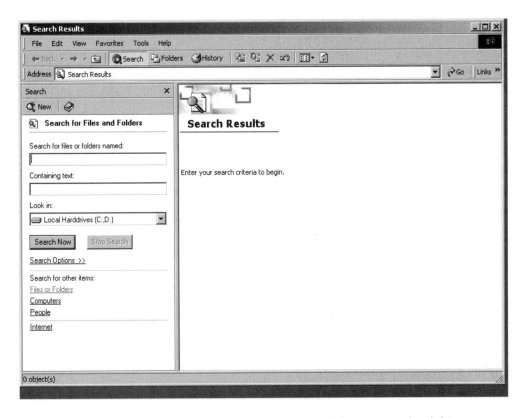

Figure 1-7 Using the Search Results dialog box to find files on your local drive or your network.

2. Enter your search criteria.

In the Search For Files Or Folders Named box, enter the part of the filename you know or, in the Containing Text box, enter a term or phrase that you know is contained in the document you want to find.

3. Begin the search.

Click Search Now. You'll see the results of your search in the pane on the right.

To search for information on the Internet, you need to be connected to the Internet. These details are discussed in Skill 6.

NOTE *In Windows 98 or Windows 95, the Search command is called Find.*

Getting help

When you're stumped about how to do something in Windows 2000 Professional, you can always track down the office computer guru and ask her. But what if she's busy or, worse, not at work? Click the Start button, and then click Help to open the Windows 2000 Professional Help system, which is shown in Figure 1-8.

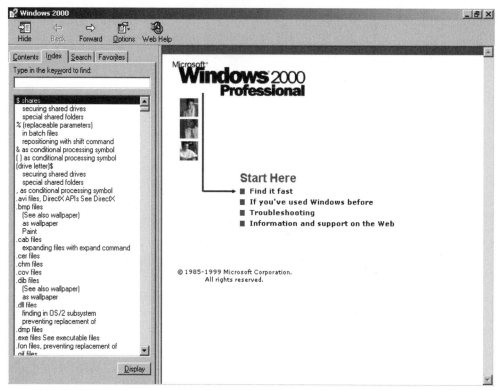

Figure 1-8   Getting help in Windows 2000 Professional.

Figure 1-8 shows Help open to the Index tab. To get help with something, enter a term in the Type In The Keyword To Find box. As you type, the list scrolls to the alphabetic area that matches what you've entered so far. When you see the topic that corresponds to your entry, double-click it to open it in the pane on the right.

Click the Contents tab to display a sort of Table of Contents for Help. Click the book icon next to a topic to display still more topics, and then click a topic to display its contents in the right pane.

Click the Search tab to find help with something that doesn't appear on the Contents tab or that you couldn't find using the Index tab. When you enter a term in the Search tab, you search the contents of everything in Help, and Help displays a list of articles that contain the term you entered.

If you find an article you might want to access again or frequently, click the Favorites tab, and click the Add button to place it on the list. When you then want to revisit the topic, you can simply select it from the Favorites list rather than search for it.

TIP   *If you've been a Windows 98, Windows 95, or Windows NT Workstation user, click the If You've Used Windows Before link on the opening Help screen. You'll see a list of components in these earlier versions of Windows that have new names or new locations in Windows 2000 Professional. Click the name of a component to display information about where it is or what it's called in Windows 2000 Professional.*

Using the Run dialog box

Windows 2000 Professional almost always has more than one way to do something—start a program, open a document, or go to an Internet site, for example. Although the Run dialog box might not necessarily be your first choice, it is one of the many tools at your disposal for accessing programs, documents, folders, and Internet sites. Click Start, and then click Run to open the Run dialog box, as shown in Figure 1-9.

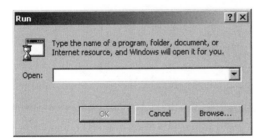

Figure 1-9   The Run dialog box.

To open a resource, you can type its name in the Open box, or you can click Browse to look for it.

Logging off and shutting down

One of the most important features of Windows 2000 Professional is security. But you have to use security features properly in order to protect your system and the valuable information you store on it. For example, you're working on a document that concerns an employee's compensation. It's in a folder on your network drive that you have access to, and it's open on your screen. You're not quite finished with it, but it's almost noon, and somebody drops by to see whether you're interested in going to lunch. You close the document, grab your coat, and take off.

Now, you are still logged on to your computer and the network, and anybody who cares to can sit down at your computer and open that document or any others to which you have access. If you log off before you leave for lunch, somebody has to know your username and password to get back onto your system and mess with your files. To log off, click Start, and then click Shut Down to open the Shut Down Windows dialog box, as shown in Figure 1-10. When you select Log Off from the drop-down list and then click OK, you end your current session and leave the computer running.

Figure 1-10   Logging off Windows 2000 Professional.

Depending on which features your hardware supports and which power options you enable, you will see any or all the following options in addition to Log Off:

- Standby turns off your monitor, hard disk, and potentially other devices to conserve power. When you start to use your computer again, it comes to life quickly, and the desktop looks just as it did when you went on standby (unless there is a power failure).

- Hibernate shuts down your computer after saving everything in memory to your hard drive. The computer is completely off when in Hibernation mode.

- Shut Down powers down your computer.

- Restart restarts the system. You often choose Restart when you are dual-booting Windows 2000 Professional and another operating system and you want to close Windows 2000 Professional and boot the other system.

- Disconnect appears on the drop-down list only if you are connected to a Windows 2000 Server that is running Terminal Services.

You'll find out soon enough, if you haven't already, that it's to your advantage to shut down the system properly. If you don't, the next time you start up, you'll have to wait while Windows 2000 Professional does some file checking and some maintenance, and you might even lose some data or some configuration settings.

TIP   *A common misconception is that you're in less danger of losing data on a computer if you just keep it running all the time. Although this statement was true in the past, today's machines are built so that you risk nothing by powering them down when you're ready for bed or ready to leave the office. You might also find that your office is much more comfortable in the morning if your computers were shut down the night before. Computers generate a substantial amount of heat; if you live in a hot climate, the longer they are up and running, the more you're tempted to crank down the thermostat on your AC.*

Using the Taskbar

The *taskbar* is the toolbar at the bottom of the desktop, and it's divided into the Quick Launch toolbar and the status area. Figure 1-11 shows the taskbar on my system.

Figure 1-11   The taskbar in Windows 2000 Professional.

Accessing the Quick Launch toolbar

You'll see right away that clicking an item on the taskbar is your fastest route to any running program. When you are using an application (for example, Microsoft Word) and you minimize it, its icon appears on the Quick Launch toolbar. To reopen the application, simply click its icon.

You can also start Internet Explorer and Outlook Express by clicking their icons on the Quick Launch toolbar. If you have multiple windows open and you need to access something on your desktop, click the Show Desktop icon to minimize all open windows and display the desktop. For this concept to work, you must be able to see the taskbar. Later, this section discusses hiding and displaying the taskbar.

Using the status area

If you are connected to a corporate network that has upgraded from Windows NT to Windows 2000, you'll probably hear the status area referred to as the system tray. Regardless of what it's called, the status area contains, by default, the Volume icon and the clock, or the time. If you hover the mouse cursor over the time, the current date is displayed. You might also see icons for other currently running services on your system, such as Task Scheduler.

To change the date or time, double-click the time to open the Date/Time Properties dialog box. To lower or raise the volume of your speakers, click the Volume icon once to display a slider bar and the Mute check box. To fine-tune your system's sounds, double-click the Volume icon to open the Volume Control dialog box, as shown in Figure 1-12. Use the slider bars to adjust volume and balance, and click the Mute All check box to silence your computer.

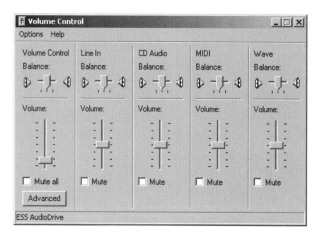

Figure 1-12   The Volume Control dialog box.

TIP   *If you acquired your keyboard recently, you might have keyboard buttons you can press to raise and lower the volume as well as to mute your computer. And, of course, you can always use the volume knob on your speakers. If you work in an office with several others, you might want to make silencing the default sounds that accompany Windows events one of your first tasks when you start up a new system. If you decide to play a CD, though, you'll need to remember to turn the sound back on.*

Hiding and displaying the taskbar

You can completely hide the taskbar, always display it, or choose to hide it unless you point to it. To hide the taskbar completely, click its top edge, and then drag the top edge down to the bottom edge. To display it once again, drag the visible edge upward.

To specify how and when the taskbar is displayed, right-click an empty area of the taskbar, and choose Properties from the shortcut menu to open the Taskbar And Start Menu Properties dialog box, as shown in Figure 1-13.

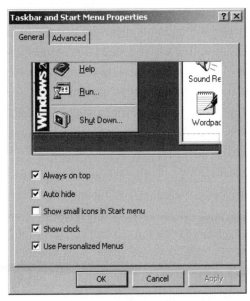

Figure 1-13   The Taskbar And Start Menu Properties dialog box

If you want the taskbar visible at all times, even when you are working in an application program and have it maximized, click the Always On Top check box only. If you want the taskbar hidden unless you point to it, select both the Always On Top check box and the Auto Hide check box.

TIP *To add a toolbar to the taskbar, right-click an empty area of the taskbar, and choose Address, Links, or Desktop from the shortcut menu. To remove a toolbar from the taskbar, select it again (to remove the check mark) from the shortcut menu.*

Using the Desktop Icons

When you first install Windows 2000 Professional, you'll see five icons on the desktop. These are shortcuts that point to the My Documents folder, the My Computer folder, the My Network Places folder, the Recycle Bin folder, and Internet Explorer. A *shortcut* is a representation of a tool or a program; it is not the real thing. When you remove a shortcut, you remove only the representation—not the actual program or file. You can remove the My Documents shortcut and the Internet Explorer shortcut, but you cannot remove the other default desktop shortcuts. You can remove any other shortcuts you place on the desktop. Later in this skill, you read about how to create shortcuts.

If you bought your Windows 2000 Professional computer with the operating system already installed, you might find a number of shortcuts on the desktop. Many might point to programs or tools that you never plan to use or that you certainly don't want cluttering up your desktop. To remove the shortcut, you can simply click it and drag it to the Recycle Bin. To remove the program or tool itself, you have to use the Add/Remove Programs applet in Control Panel. Skill 5 shows you how.

NOTE *To rearrange the icons on your desktop, simply click an icon and drag it to a new location.*

My Documents

Double-clicking My Documents opens the My Documents folder, as shown in Figure 1-14. By default, the My Documents folder contains only the My Pictures folder, which you can use to store graphics images. In Figure 1-14, you'll also see a Fax folder, which was created when the Windows 2000 Professional Fax services was installed.

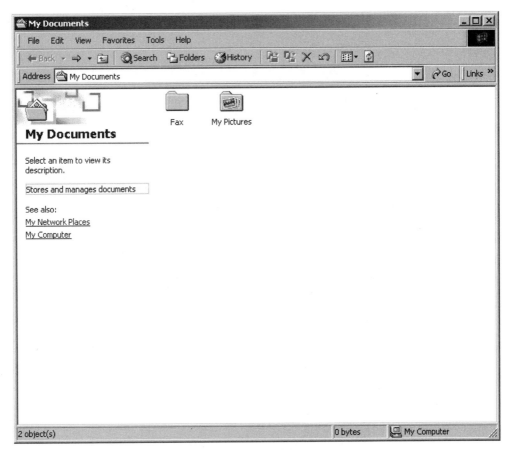

Figure 1-14   The My Documents folder

Double-click a folder to display its contents. When you select a folder, information about its contents is displayed on the left. Click the Back or Forward button to move from file to folder view.

The My Documents folder also contains links to the My Network Places folder and the My Computer folder on the left side of the window. Click a link to open that folder.

My Computer

Double-clicking My Computer opens the My Computer folder, as shown in Figure 1-15. This folder is a window into your local computer. From here, you can navigate to any disk, any program, any folder, or any file, for example. In a sense, this is an overview of what you see in Windows Explorer. (Windows Explorer is discussed in the next skill.)

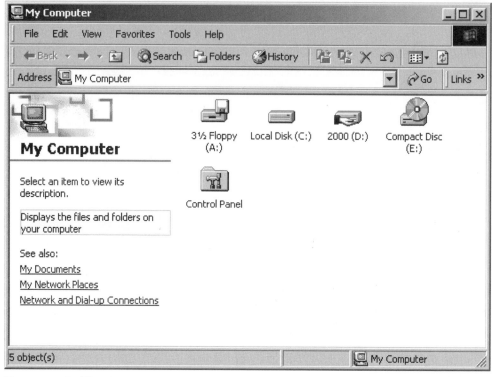

Figure 1-15 The My Computer folder.

Click an icon to display its contents. When you select an icon, information about the item is displayed in the left pane. For example, if you click the icon for a drive, the left pane displays the amount of free and used space both numerically and graphically.

TIP *To display information about your computer system or any system component, right-click the My Computer icon on the desktop, and choose Properties to open the System Properties dialog box.*

My Network Places

Double-clicking My Network Places opens the My Network Places folder (see Figure 1-16), which is a window on your local area network. You use the options in this folder to set up and use your network. Skill 4 looks at this folder in detail.

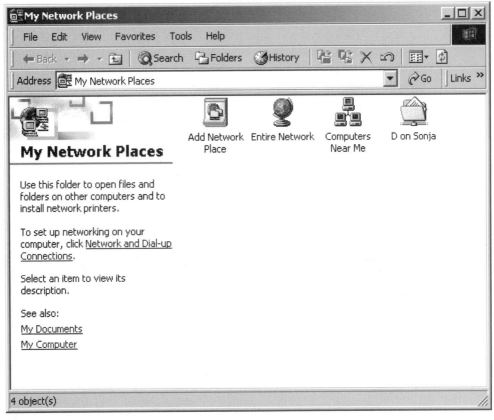

Figure 1-16 The My Network Places folder.

NOTE *In previous versions of Windows, My Network Places was called Network Neighborhood.*

Recycle Bin

When you delete a file or a folder in Windows 2000 Professional, it's not really removed from your hard drive—it goes to the Recycle Bin. The Recycle Bin is a safety net because you can, up to a point, retrieve items from the Recycle Bin. By default, the Recycle Bin is set to exist on 10 percent of each drive on your system. When the Recycle Bin is full, the oldest files in the Recycle Bin are automatically deleted to make room for other files. Until this point or until you manually empty the Recycle Bin, you can retrieve a file or folder. To do so, follow these steps:

WARNING *Files that you delete from floppy disks, Zip disks, and network drives are immediately deleted—they don't go to the Recycle Bin first.*

1. Open the Recycle Bin folder.

Double-click the Recycle Bin icon on the desktop. You'll see something similar to what's shown in Figure 1-17.

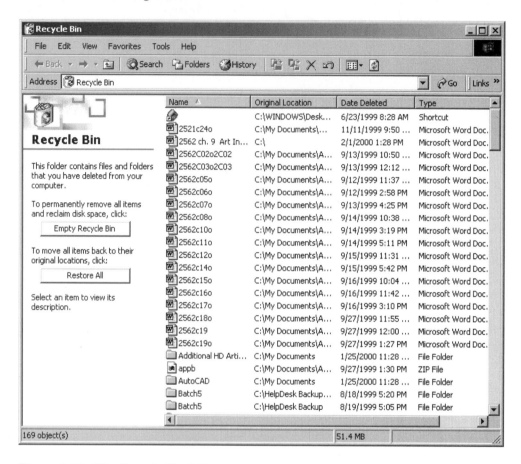

Figure 1-17   The Recycle Bin folder.

2. Retrieve the file or folder.

Select the file or folder you want to retrieve, and then click the Restore button to send it back to its original location.

To empty the Recycle Bin manually, click the Empty Recycle Bin button.

To bypass the Recycle Bin and remove files and folders immediately when you choose or press Delete, follow these steps:

1. Open the Recycle Bin Properties dialog box (see Figure 1-18).

Right-click the Recycle Bin icon on the desktop, and choose Properties from the shortcut menu.

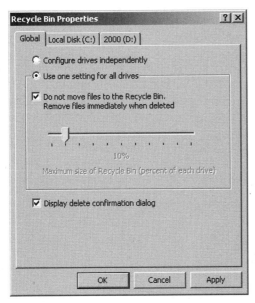

Figure 1-18   The Recycle Bin Properties dialog box.

2. Specify that items not be moved to the Recycle Bin.

Click the Global tab, and then click the Do Not Move Files To The Recycle Bin check box.

3. Close the Recycle Bin Properties dialog box.

Click OK.

TIP   *To change the size of the Recycle Bin, move the slider on the Global tab in the Recycle Bin Properties dialog box.*

Internet Explorer

Internet Explorer 5 is the Web browser that comes with Windows 2000 Professional. You can open it in several ways:

- Double-click the shortcut on the desktop.

- Click the Launch Internet Explorer Browser icon on the taskbar.

- Click a link to a Web page in any document.

Skill 6 discusses Internet Explorer in detail.

Connect To The Internet

When you first install Windows 2000 Professional (and before you set up an Internet connection), you'll have a Connect To The Internet icon on your desktop. Click this icon to start the Internet Connection Wizard, as shown in Figure 1-19. You can use this wizard to sign up for a new Internet account, transfer an existing account, or set up an Internet connection through your local area network.

Figure 1-19 Using the Internet Connection Wizard to set up a connection to the Internet.

Using and Creating Shortcuts

Because shortcuts have been mentioned several times in this skill, you might have the impression that they are handy devices, and they are indeed. You can create a shortcut on the desktop to just about anything you want to access easily and frequently—Web sites, files, folders, programs, or Windows Explorer, for example. Sometimes when you install an application, the application's setup program even places a shortcut to the application on the desktop.

To create a shortcut for an item you can see, follow these steps:

1. Open the Programs menu (or any other menu).

Click the Start button, and then click Programs.

2. Create the shortcut.

Right-click the item, and drag it to the desktop. From the shortcut menu that appears, select Create Shortcut(s) Here.

To create a shortcut for an item you can't see, follow these steps:

1. Start the Create Shortcut Wizard, which is shown in Figure 1-20.

Right-click an empty area of the desktop, click New, and then click Shortcut.

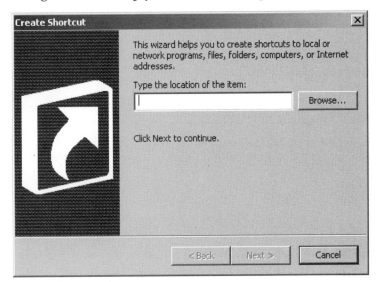

Figure 1-20 The Create Shortcut Wizard.

2. Identify the item.

In the Type The Location Of The Item box, enter the path for the item, or click Browse to find it.

3. Give the item a name.

Click Next to open the Select A Title For The Program screen, and in the Type A Name For This Shortcut box, enter a name.

4. Close the Wizard.

Click Finish to close the Wizard and create the shortcut on the desktop.

To delete a shortcut, you can drag it to the Recycle Bin or right-click it and choose Delete from the shortcut menu. To rename a shortcut, right-click it, choose Rename from the shortcut menu, type the new name, and then click outside the name box.

You can change the icons associated with some shortcuts. To do so, follow these steps:

1. Open the Properties dialog box for the icon.

Right-click the icon, and choose Properties from the shortcut menu.

2. Open the Change Icon dialog box, which is shown in Figure 1-21.

Click the Change Icon button.

Figure 1-21 The Change Icon dialog box.

3. Select a new icon.

Click a new icon, and then click OK.

NOTE *If you don't see a Change Icon button in the Properties dialog box for an icon, you can't change the icon associated with that item.*

Tips for Users of Previous Versions of Windows

If you've used previous versions of Windows—Windows NT Workstation 4, Windows 98, or Windows 95—you might be slightly bewildered when you take some action that's second nature and get nothing or find yourself somewhere other than where you wanted to be. Here are some tips to ease the transition to Windows 2000 Professional:

- Add New Hardware has been renamed to Add/Remove Hardware. It's still located in Control Panel.

- Windows NT's Devices applet has been replaced by Device Manager—ala Windows 98 and Windows 95. To open it, right-click My Computer and choose Properties to open the System Properties dialog box. Click the Hardware tab, and then click the Device Manager button.

- Dial-Up Networking has been renamed Network And Dial-Up Connections and is located in Control Panel.

- Favorites in not on the Start menu. To add it, right-click an empty area of the taskbar, and choose Properties from the shortcut menu to open the Taskbar And Start Menu Properties dialog box. Click the Advanced tab, and in the Start Menu Settings list, click the Display Favorites check box.

- The MS-DOS prompt has been renamed Command Prompt and is on the Accessories menu. To open the Accessories menu, click Start, click Programs, and then click Accessories.

- Options has been renamed Folder Options and is on the Tools menu in many places, including the My Computer folder, the My Network Places folder, and Control Panel.

- Power Management has been renamed Power Options and is located in Control Panel.

- User Manager has been renamed Local Users And Groups and is located in Control Panel.

Summary

This skill took you on a brisk tour of what you see when you start up Windows 2000 Professional. Now you can log on and off successfully, create a strong password, access the items on the Start menu, use the taskbar to navigate quickly and easily among running programs, open the folders represented by the icons on the desktop, and use, create, and remove shortcuts as well as change the icon associated with shortcuts.

Skill 2

MANAGE FILES AND FOLDERS

Featuring:

- Understanding File Systems in Windows 2000 Professional
- Organizing Documents in Windows Explorer
- Setting File and Folder Permissions
- Working with Offline Files
- Specifying Folder Options
- Backing Up and Restoring Files and Folders

I've always been fascinated with people's work styles—how they decorate their offices, how they organize their files, what they keep on the top of their desks, what kinds of notes are posted on their computer monitors, for example. It seems to me that all these things tell you a great deal about how a person thinks and works. But does a messy office indicate a fuzzy head? Not necessarily. Some of the most efficient businesspeople I know need a guide and a map to find their briefcase when they shut down for the day.

How you organize your office, though, is probably a pretty good indication of how you organize the information you keep on your computer. My main point here is that it doesn't matter much what kind of system you impose as long as you have a system that lets you get at stuff easily and quickly. Not knowing where you've saved a document and using the Search command every time you want to work on something is a system, but it's not a system that lets you find stuff easily and quickly. Understanding Windows Explorer and knowing how to use it to organize your programs and documents is an efficient system for quickly and easily retrieving what you need.

While I'm on my soapbox here, I'm continually amazed at the number of people who work all day every day on their computer and don't know a thing about Windows Explorer. If you're a busy professional, you'll do yourself a huge favor by taking a few minutes to get on speaking terms with Windows Explorer. In fact, this information alone will probably save you in time and aggravation many times the cost of this book.

This skill starts by explaining the types of file systems that Windows 2000 Professional can use. If you've used previous versions of Windows and have recently upgraded to Windows 2000 Professional, you now have a new option as far as file systems are concerned. Next, you read step by step how to manage your files and folders using Windows Explorer, which, of course, is the heart of the matter. This skill then quickly looks at how to use offline files, how to use the Folder Options dialog box to display the kind of information you want, and how to back up and restore files and folders.

NOTE   *If your eyes start to glaze over after you read the first paragraph in the next section, try to keep going. Some technical-sounding terms are necessary, but they're followed by explanations, and, besides, they aren't that difficult to understand. If you plan to set up a network in your office (or at home), you'll need to have a handle on this stuff before you install Windows 2000 Professional.*

Understanding File Systems in Windows 2000 Professional

A *file system* in an operating system is the overall structure that determines how files are named, stored, and organized. When you install Windows 2000 Professional, you can choose to use any of three file systems:

- *FAT* stands for File Allocation Table, the file system supported by DOS, Windows 3.*x,* and Windows 95 release 1. Sometimes referred to as FAT16, this is a 16-bit file system.

- *FAT32* stands for File Allocation Table 32, the file system supported by Windows 95 release 2, Windows 98, and Windows Me.

- *NTFS* stands for New Technology File System, the file system supported by Windows NT.

Which system you choose depends in part on the size of your hard drive, how you plan to set up your network (if you intend to network your computers), and how secure you want your system to be.

The FAT file system

In the FAT approach to organizing your files, a database (the File Allocation Table) is created at the beginning of your hard drive. When you store a file on your hard drive, the operating system places information about it in the FAT so that you can later retrieve the file when you want it. You cannot use the FAT file system with a disk larger than 4 gigabytes. While the FAT file system uses the 8.3 file-naming convention under the hood (that is, a file's name can be a maximum of eight letters), beginning with Windows 95 and Windows NT 3.5, long filenames are supported on FAT disks. The three letters following the period are the file *extension*, which identifies the file's type.

The FAT32 file system

The FAT32 file system evolved from the FAT file system. Because of the way FAT32 is structured, however, you can use it with a hard drive as large as 2 terabytes. FAT32 also uses space on your hard drive much more efficiently. A few years ago when I converted a FAT drive to FAT32, I almost doubled the space available on the drive. In addition, the FAT32 system lets you use long filenames; the maximum is 255 characters. The FAT32 file system is therefore a much better choice than FAT.

The NTFS file system

Although you can use the FAT and FAT32 file systems with Windows 2000 Professional, I recommend that you use NTFS, for these following reasons:

- It has many security features, including password protection for files and folders.

- It provides better disk compression and file encryption. In other words, you can store more in less space, and you can encode data to prevent unauthorized access.

- You can use NTFS on a hard drive as large as 2 terabytes, and performance does not degrade as drive size increases.

- It provides better protection from viruses. Most viruses are written to attack systems formatted to FAT and FAT32, and they don't know what to do when they encounter NTFS.

- NTFS creates a backup of the Master File Table (MFT), which is the equivalent of the FAT database. If the boot sector of your hard drive becomes damaged, you can replace the information from the backup.

NOTE   *A Windows 2000 Professional installation that uses NTFS can see and access FAT and FAT32 files.*

Knowing which file system is best for you

One size does not fit all when selecting a file system, so here are some guidelines:

- If you are installing Windows 2000 Professional on a standalone system or on a network that includes only Windows 2000 machines (Windows 2000 Server or Professional), choose NTFS. It is a robust, secure file system and it is your best bet if you want the additional features.

- If you are setting up a dual-boot configuration, for example, in which one partition uses Windows 98 and the other uses Windows 2000 Professional and it is important that each operating system be able to see the other's files, use FAT or FAT32.

- If you are setting up a dual-boot configuration with Windows NT you either need to use FAT or make sure that Windows NT is version 4 running Service Pack 5 or later (otherwise Windows NT won't be able to access any partitions that have been accessed by Windows 2000).

Organizing Documents in Windows Explorer

Regardless of the file system you are using, Windows Explorer is your tool of choice for imposing a sense of organization on your documents. From the desktop, you can open Windows Explorer in the following ways:

- Click the Start button, click Programs, click Accessories, and then click Windows Explorer.

- Right-click My Documents, My Computer, My Network Places, or Recycle Bin, and choose Explore from the shortcut menu.

You'll see something similar to Figure 2-1.

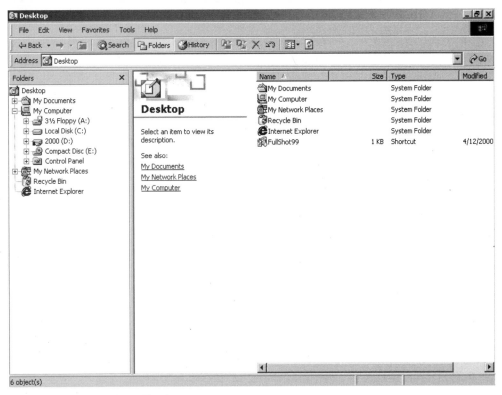

Figure 2-1 Windows Explorer.

In the Folders pane, select a folder to display its contents in the right pane. Click the plus sign (+) next to an item to display a list of what it contains. In the right pane, double-click a folder to display its subfolders or files. If you can't see all the items in the pane, drag the horizontal scroll bar to the right or drag the vertical scroll bar up or down.

Opening files and folders

To open any file or folder in Windows Explorer, simply double-click it. As discussed in Skill 1, in most cases the file or folder will open in the application in which it was created. To open a file on your network, follow these steps:

1. Navigate to My Network Places.

In the Folders pane, scroll down to My Network Places.

2. Find the file you want to open.

Expand My Network Places, click the disk, click the folder, and then double-click the filename to open the file.

Creating folders

Whether you're working on a standalone Windows 2000 Professional machine or on a network, you have a user folder that was created during installation. You'll find that folder in the Documents And Settings folder. Inside your user folder is a My Documents folder. Although you can create a folder just about anywhere you want in the folder hierarchy, I suggest for starters that you keep your documents in subfolders of the My Documents folder. If you are on a corporate network, that might be the only place you have permission to store documents, or your system administrator might have created a folder on a specific drive for you.

I create subfolders for each of my projects in my My Documents folder, and then sometimes I create sub-subfolders and store documents in those. For example, I have a folder in the My Documents folder for this book, and then within that folder I have subfolders for each skill. In that subfolder, I keep the art files and the document files I create for each skill.

You can create a folder from the desktop, from within Windows Explorer, and from within a Windows application.

Creating a folder on the desktop

To create a folder on the desktop, follow these steps:

1. **Create a folder.**

   Right-click an empty area on the desktop, choose New from the shortcut menu, and then click Folder. You'll see a folder icon on the desktop and a box beneath it containing the words *New Folder*.

2. **Name the folder.**

   Type a name for the new folder, and then click outside the box.

Your new folder will be stored in the Desktop subfolder in your username folder. You can leave it there or move it, as you'll see later in this section.

Creating a folder from within Windows Explorer

To create a folder inside another folder in Windows Explorer, follow these steps:

1. **Locate the parent folder.**

   Expand a folder or navigate to the folder inside which you want to create a new folder.

2. Use the commands on the File menu to create the folder.

Click the File menu, click New, and then click Folder. You'll see a folder icon in the right pane and a box beneath it that contains the words *New Folder*, as shown in Figure 2-2.

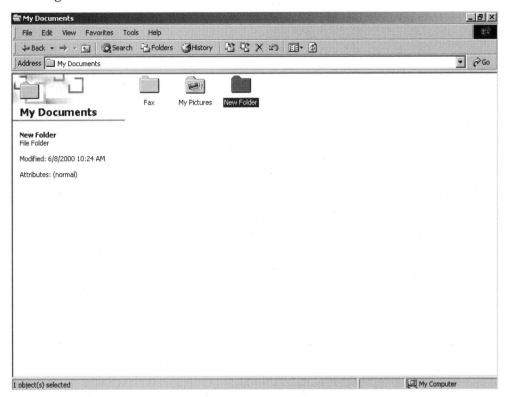

Figure 2-2 Creating a new folder in Windows Explorer.

3. Give the folder a name.

Type a name for the folder, and then click outside the box.

Creating a folder from within an application

This method is often the handiest way to create a folder. Follow these steps for creating a folder in WordPad, an application that is included with Windows 2000 Professional, although a similar procedure works in most Windows applications:

1. Open WordPad.

Click the Start button, click Programs, click Accessories, and then click WordPad. Figure 2-3 shows WordPad open with a blank document screen.

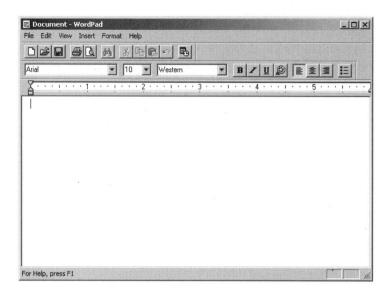

Figure 2-3 WordPad, a word-processing application that comes with Windows 2000 Professional.

2. Open the Save As dialog box.

Click the File menu, and then click Save. Figure 2-4 shows the Save As dialog box.

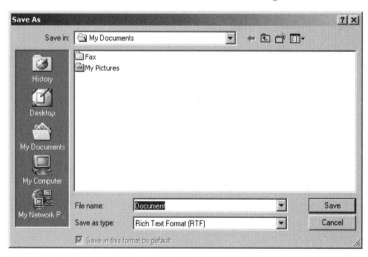

Figure 2-4 The Save As dialog box.

3. Create the folder.

Locate the folder in which you want to create the new folder, and then click the Create New Folder button. You'll see a new folder icon followed by a box that contains the words *New Folder.*

4. Name the folder.

Type a name for your folder, and then click outside the box.

Naming files and folders

In Windows 2000 Professional, a filename or a folder name can contain a maximum of 215 characters, but because most programs can't deal with names of that length, you should use fewer characters. Filenames and folder names can include spaces, commas, semicolons, equal signs, and square brackets and can be a combination of upper- and lowercase letters.

Be sure to give your files and folders names that are descriptive and that will make sense sometime in the future when you're trying to locate something in particular.

Creating files

As with folders, you can create files in three ways: from the desktop, from within Windows Explorer, and from within a Windows application.

Creating a file on the desktop

To create a file on the desktop, follow these steps:

1. Open a shortcut menu.

Right-click an empty area on the desktop, click New, and then click the type of file you want to create. You'll see an icon on the desktop and a box beneath it containing the words *New [application] Document*.

2. Name the file.

Type a name for the new file, and then click outside the box.

This file is stored in the desktop folder in your username folder.

In Windows 2000 Professional, each file has an extension that identifies its type. For example, if you create a text document in WordPad, the extension is TXT. To see a file's extension in Windows Explorer, click the View menu, and then choose Details.

Creating a file in Windows Explorer

To create a file in Windows Explorer, follow these steps:

1. Open Windows Explorer.

Right-click the My Computer icon, and choose Explore from the shortcut menu.

2. Select a folder.

Open the folder that will contain the new file.

3. Create the file.

Click the File menu, click New, and then select a file type. You'll see an icon representing the file type and a box in the right pane.

4. Name the file.

Type a name for the new file, and then click outside the box.

Creating a file from within an application

Follow these steps to create a file in WordPad. You use the same procedure to create a file in any Windows application:

1. Open WordPad.

Click the Start button, click Programs, click Accessories, and then click WordPad.

2. Open the Save As dialog box.

Click the File menu, and then click Save.

3. Choose where you want to store the file.

Click the folder in which you want to save the file you're creating.

4. Name and save the file.

In the File Name box, enter a name for the file, and then select the file type in the Save As Type dialog box. Click Save.

Copying and moving files and folders

As mentioned earlier in this skill, regardless of where you create a file or a folder, you can always move it to another location. In addition, you can copy it to another location. When you move a file, you remove it from its current location and place it in another location. When you copy a file, the original remains in place, and a copy is placed in another location.

As with a number of tasks in Windows 2000 Professional, you can move and copy a file or a folder in several ways:

- Drag and drop with the right mouse button.

- Drag and drop with the left mouse button.

- Copy and paste or cut and paste.

- Use the Send To command.

Which method you use depends on the situation and your personal preference.

Using the right mouse button

To copy or move a file or a folder with the right mouse button, follow these steps:

1. **Open Windows Explorer.**

   Right-click the My Computer icon, and choose Explore from the shortcut menu.

2. **Drag the file to its new location.**

   Locate the file or folder, right-click it, and, while holding down the mouse button, drag the file or folder to its new location.

3. **Choose whether to copy or move the file or folder.**

   Release the right mouse, and choose Copy Here or Move Here from the shortcut menu.

If you change your mind in the middle of a copy or a move, press the Escape key.

Using the left mouse button

If the source and destination for a copy are on different drives, left-click the file, and then drag it to its new location. If the source and destination are on the same drive, left-clicking and dragging the file or folder moves it. To move a file or a folder to a different drive, click the file or folder with the left mouse button, and hold down the Shift key while you drag the item.

Using the Cut, Copy, and Paste commands

To copy or move a file using the Cut, Copy, and Paste commands, follow these steps:

1. **Open Windows Explorer.**

   Right-click the My Computer icon, and choose Explore from the shortcut menu.

2. **Locate what you want to copy or move.**

   Find the source file or folder.

3. **Open the shortcut menu.**

   Right-click the source file or folder, and choose Cut or Copy from the shortcut menu.

4. Place the item in its new location.

Right-click the destination folder, and choose Paste from the shortcut menu.

Using the Send To command

A quick way to copy files and folders is to use the Send To command, which is on the shortcut menu. Simply right-click the file or folder, choose Send To, and then select a destination. By default, you can send a file or a folder to a floppy disk, the desktop, a mail recipient, or the My Documents folder.

If you frequently want to copy files to a destination that's not on the Send To menu, you can add that destination. For example, you might want to back up your files on another computer's hard drive on your network. To add a destination to the Send To menu, follow these steps:

1. Open Windows Explorer.

Right-click the My Computer icon, and choose Explore from the shortcut menu.

2. Find your Send To folder.

Locate your username folder, and then locate your Send To folder within it.

TIP   *If you don't see your Send To folder, it's probably hidden. To display it, click the Tools menu, choose Folder Options to open the Folder Options dialog box, click the View tab, click the Show Hidden File And Folder option on the Advanced Settings list, and then click OK.*

3. Start the Create Shortcut Wizard, which is shown in Figure 2-5.

Click the File menu, click New, and then click Shortcut.

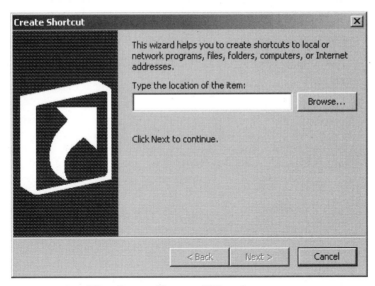

Figure 2-5   The Create Shortcut Wizard.

4. Enter the destination you want to add.

In the Type The Location Of The Item box, enter the filename for your new destination, or click Browse to locate it.

5. Enter a name for the destination.

Click Next, and, on the Select A Title For The Program screen, type a name for the destination. Click Finish.

TIP   *The Send To command is also on the File menu in many Windows 2000 applications.*

Renaming files and folders

Renaming files and folders is simple. In Windows Explorer, right-click a file or a folder, choose Rename from the shortcut menu, type a new name in the box that appears, and then click outside the box. You can also rename a file or a folder from within a Windows application. Open the Save As dialog box, right-click the file or folder, choose Rename from the shortcut menu, type a new name, and click outside the box.

Deleting files and folders

As mentioned in Skill 1, whenever you delete a file or a folder, it goes to the Recycle Bin by default. The file or folder is not permanently deleted from your system until the Recycle Bin is emptied. You can delete a file or folder in several ways:

- In Windows Explorer, right-click the file or folder name, and choose Delete from the shortcut menu.

- In the Save As dialog box in a Windows 2000 Professional application, right-click the name of a file or a folder, and choose Delete from the shortcut menu.

- In Windows Explorer, left-click the file or folder name, and then press the Delete key or click the Delete button on the toolbar. (The Delete button has an X on it.)

- If the file or folder is visible on the desktop, click it, and then drag it to the Recycle Bin.

TIP   *To bypass the Recycle Bin, hold down the Shift key while choosing the Delete command or pressing the Delete key.*

Finding files and folders

If you follow the guidelines in this chapter, you shouldn't lose track of the documents, file, and folders you create—although we all do from time to time. In that situation, you can use the Search command to look for a file, a folder, or text within a document. You can start a search in the following ways:

- Right-click the Start button, and click Search.

- Click the Start button, click Search, and then click For Files Or Folders.

- In Windows Explorer, click the Search button on the toolbar.

- In any Windows Explorer-like window, right-click an item, and choose Search from the shortcut menu.

Figure 2-6 shows the Search Results dialog box. The Search Options button was clicked to display more of the options in the Search pane.

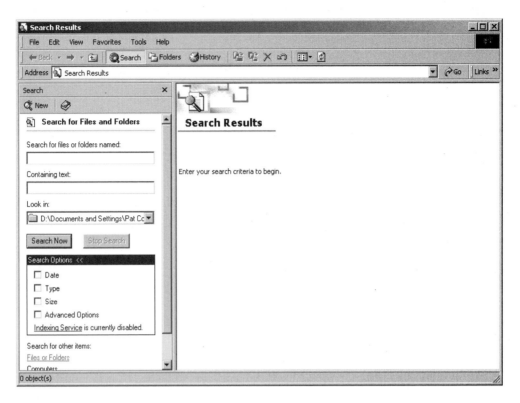

Figure 2-6 The Search Results dialog box.

To find a file if you remember its name or part of its name, follow these steps:

1. Specify what you want to find.

In the Search For Files Or Folders Named box, enter the file's name or part of the name. If you want to search the contents of files for a particular term or phrase, enter that information in the Containing Text box.

2. Specify more criteria if you want.

If you want to search for files that were created or modified during a certain period, for files of a certain size or type, or to further refine your search, click the Search Options link to open the Search Options section of the dialog box, as shown in Figure 2-7.

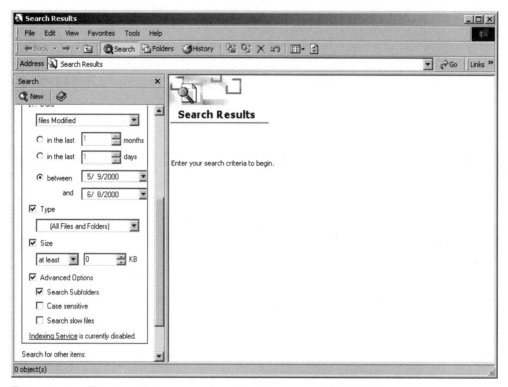

Figure 2-7   Further refining a search in the Search Results dialog box.

3. Start the search.

When you have specified all your options, click Search Now. The results of your search are displayed in the right pane.

When you're searching, you can use wildcard characters to represent unknowns. For example, if you want to find all the document files, enter *.doc as your search term. The asterisk represents one or more characters. Use the question mark to represent a single unknown character.

If your computer system contains hundreds or perhaps thousands of files, you might want to investigate using Indexing Service. This program reads through files and extracts the text and properties and then places them in an index. Searching the index that is created is much faster and more powerful than searching the files themselves.

Indexing Service is not enabled by default. To enable it, click the Indexing Service link in the Search Results dialog box to open the Indexing Service Settings dialog box, as shown in Figure 2-8.

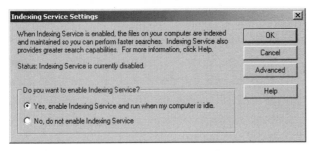

Figure 2-8   Enabling the Indexing Service.

If you're on a corporate network, see your system administrator about enabling and using Indexing Service. For more information about Indexing Service, click the Advanced button in the Indexing Service Settings dialog box to open the Indexing Service console, click the Action menu, and then click Help.

Setting File and Folder Permissions

As this book continues to point out, one of the reasons you choose to use Windows 2000 Professional is its security features. You can restrict access to your system right down to the file and folder level if you are using the NTFS file system. Even if someone walks into your office and makes off with your computer, they won't be able to access the files and folders unless they have permission.

Assigning permissions to a file or folder is a straightforward process, so this section looks at the steps to do that first. Understanding the types of permissions you can assign is a bit more complicated, and the next section gives you a brief rundown on that subject.

To assign permissions to a file or a folder, follow these steps:

1. **Open Windows Explorer.**

    Right-click the My Computer icon, and choose Explore from the shortcut menu.

2. **Specify the file or folder to which you want to attach permissions.**

    Right-click the file or folder, and choose Properties from the shortcut menu to open the Properties dialog box for that folder. Click the Security tab, which is shown in Figure 2-9.

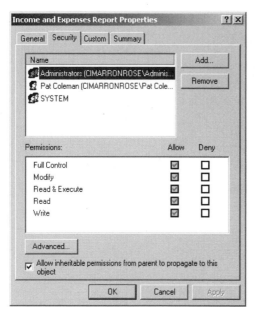

Figure 2-9   The Security tab in the Properties dialog box.

3. Specify who can have access to this file.

Click Add to open the Select Users, Computers, Or Groups dialog box, as shown in Figure 2-10. Select the groups to whom you want to give permission, clicking Add after each selection. When you have added all the groups you want, click OK.

TIP   *While it's tempting to assign permissions to individual users, don't. Assign permissions to groups of users such as Administrators, Power Users, or Users, and place individual users in these groups. For example, if you set the permissions on your C: drive to give Full Control to the Administrators group, and you create a new user account Susan, who is a member of the Administrators group, she will automatically be given Full Control permissions on your C: drive, without you being required to manually add her to the permissions. This can be a big time saver in the long run.*

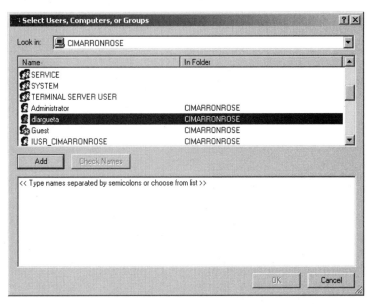

Figure 2-10 The Select Users, Computers, or Groups dialog box.

4. Specify what kinds of permissions these users will have.

Back in the Properties dialog box, you'll see that the users you specified have been added to the list. Now click the Allow or Deny check boxes to specify the type of permissions these users will have. When you're finished, click OK.

The types of permissions you can assign to files and folders are extensive, and in addition to the primary types described here, you can assign special access permissions. A discussion of special access permissions is beyond the scope of this book, but if you're interested in knowing more, check with your system administrator or look in the Windows 2000 Professional Help system.

You can assign the following primary types of permissions to files and folders:

- Read permission allows you to view the contents, permissions, and attributes associated with a file or a folder.

- Write permission allows you to create a new file or a subfolder in a folder. To change a file, you must also have Read permission.

- Read & Execute permission gives you Read and Write permissions and also allows you to pass through a folder for which you have no access to get to a file or a folder for which you do have access.

- Modify permission gives you all the permissions associated with Read & Execute and Write permissions and also gives you Delete permission.

- Full Control permission makes you king (or queen) of the hill. You have all the permissions associated with all the other permissions listed above, and you can change permissions and take ownership of files and folders. You can also delete subfolders and files even if you don't have the specific permission to do so.

Working with Offline Files

If you work on a laptop or on a network that tends to be on the slow side, you'll want to know about using offline files. When you use offline files you can work with a network or an Internet file even when you aren't connected to the network.

To make a network file available offline, follow these steps:

1. **Select the network file you want available offline.**

   On the desktop, open My Network Places, and navigate to the file you want.

2. **Start the Offline Files Wizard.**

   Right-click the file, and choose Make Available Offline. The first time you set up offline files, the Offline Files Wizard starts. After that, you'll simply see the Synchronizing dialog box.

3. **Select a synchronization option.**

   On the Wizard's Welcome screen, click Next, and then specify whether to synchronize the file with the version on the network when you log on and off your computer. Click Next.

4. **Complete the wizard.**

   On the last screen of the wizard, specify whether you want a periodic reminder that you aren't connected to the network, and elect to create a shortcut to the Offline Files folder on your desktop. Click Finish.

   The Synchronizing dialog box will show the file's progress.

Specifying Folder Options

Earlier, this skill looked briefly at using the Folder Options dialog box to display hidden files. Now it's time to take a longer look and see how you can use the options in this dialog box to specify how folders look and work. Figure 2-11 shows the Folder Options dialog box open to the General tab. To open the Folder Options dialog box, click the Tools menu, and then click Folder Options in any folder or in Windows Explorer.

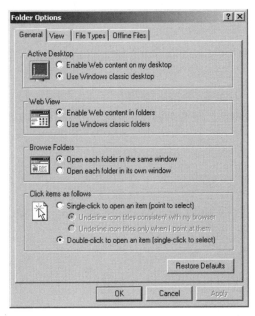

Figure 2-11   The General tab in the Folder Options dialog box.

Several of the options on this tab concern folders. Skill 5 looks at the options that concern the appearance of the desktop.

NOTE   *Changes you make in the Folder Options dialog box apply to the contents of Windows Explorer, the My Computer folder, the My Network Places folder, the My Documents folder, and Control Panel.*

Displaying folders

In the Web View section of the General tab, you can specify that folder contents are displayed as Web pages or as classic Windows folders that do not look or work like Web pages.

In the Browse Folders section, choose Open Each Folder In The Same Window if you want the window to stay put if you open a folder within another folder. Choose Open Each Folder In Its Own Window if you want a new window to appear each time you open a folder within an existing folder. Although selecting this option tends to clutter the screen, it's useful if you often want to drag and drop items between folders.

In the Click Items As Follows section, you can choose whether to single- or double-click to open items.

Specifying views

You can customize folders by applying a background image, background color, and other elements. To do so, in Windows Explorer select the folder, choose Customize This Folder from the View menu to start the Customize This Folder Wizard, and follow the onscreen instructions. After you've created your masterpiece, you can apply that look to all your folders. To do so, you use the options on the View tab of the Folder Options dialog box, which is shown in Figure 2-12.

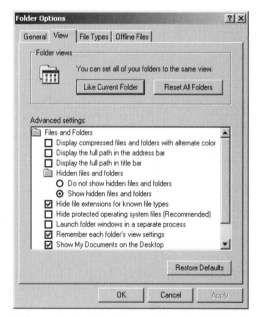

Figure 2-12 The View tab in the Folder Options dialog box.

To apply the look of a customized folder to all folders, select the folder, open the Folder Options dialog box, click the View tab, and then click the Like Current Folder button.

Scroll down the list in the Advanced Settings section of the View tab to check out the other options. For a description of each item, click the Help button (the one with the question mark), and then click the item.

Viewing file types on your system

The File Types tab, which is shown in Figure 2-13, is primarily for information only. It lists the filename extensions, their associated file type, and applications that are registered with Windows 2000 Professional. Unless you know what you are doing and have a good reason for doing it, you shouldn't experiment with this list. In fact, if you're on a corporate network, you probably don't even have permission to do so.

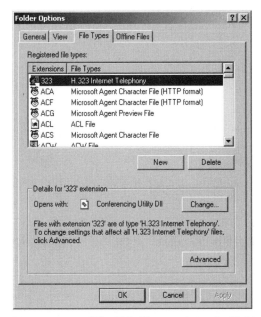

Figure 2-13   The File Types tab in the Folder Options dialog box.

Reprise: Setting up offline files

Earlier in this skill, you set up offline files using the Offline Files Wizard. You can also do this task by using the Offline Files tab in the Folder Options dialog box, which is shown in Figure 2-14.

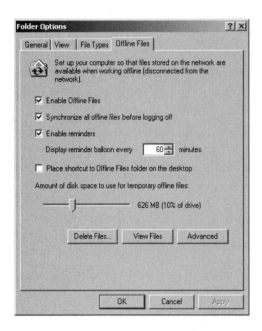

Figure 2-14 The Offline Files tab in the Folder Options dialog box.

Backing Up and Restoring Files and Folders

A *backup* is an up-to-date copy of your computer files, and the importance of backing up your files cannot be overstated. If you work on a corporate network, your system administrator has probably gone to considerable time and expense ensuring that the data on your network is backed up on a timely schedule and stored in a safe place—probably even off site.

Unfortunately, experts estimate that 95 percent of all small office/home office (SOHO) workers do not have a current backup. These same experts go so far as to say that if you don't have a current backup and you also aren't running a current version of virus protection software, don't even turn on your computer! (Later, this section talks a little about virus protection.)

You have to lose only one important document, and we all have, to become obsessed with making backups. In Windows 2000 Professional, not just anyone has backup rights. You have to be logged on as an administrator or as a backup operator, you must own the files you want to back up, or you must have one or more of the following permissions: Read, Read & Execute, Modify, Full Control.

In Windows 2000 Professional, you can back up using the Backup Wizard, or you can make a manual backup, which gives you slightly more control. This section gives you the steps for backing up both ways, looks at Web storage alternatives, discusses how to restore what you've backed up, and then talks a bit about viruses and virus protection.

A word about backup media

The medium to which you back up depends on the configuration of your hardware and peripherals. Here are some possibilities:

- If your files are small, you can back up to a floppy disk—that is, if you have a floppy drive. For security reasons, many networked computers don't have one.

- If your system includes a CD ReWritable drive and you need to back up lots of data, you can back up to a CD.

- Another possibility for storing large amounts of data is a ZIP drive, which was developed by Iomega. A ZIP drive uses 3.5-inch removable disks (ZIP disks) that can store 100 or 250 megabytes of data, depending on the type of drive you have.

- You can also back up to a tape drive if you have one. This backup medium has long been popular for corporate networks.

- If you're on a network, you can back up to a drive on another network computer.

Backing up with Backup Wizard

To use the Backup Wizard, follow these steps:

1. **Start the Backup program.**

   Click the Start button, click Programs, click Accessories, click System Tools, and then click Back. You'll see the window shown in Figure 2-15.

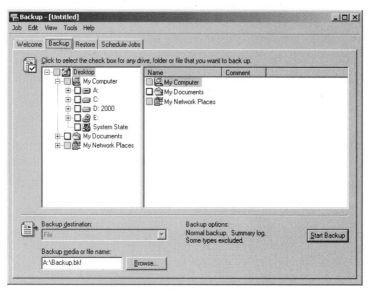

Figure 2-15   Starting Backup.

2. Start the Backup Wizard.

Click the Backup Wizard button, and, at the Welcome screen, click Next.

3. Specify what to back up.

On the What To Back Up screen, choose what you want to back up. You can back up everything on your computer; only certain files, drives, or data; or only system state information. When you've made your selection, click Next.

4. Select the items you want to back up.

On the Items To Back Up screen, which you'll see if you didn't choose to back up everything, click the items you want backed up, and then click Next.

5. Specify the destination of the backup.

On the Where To Store The Backup screen, specify the type of medium you'll be backing up to, and enter or browse for the backup's file name. Click Next.

6. Complete the wizard.

The final screen summarizes your options. To change any of them, click the Back button to return to the previous screens. If the information is correct, click Finish to start the backup. A progress indicator will track the backup as it proceeds.

Backing up manually

To back up using a more hands-on approach, click the Backup tab in the Backup window, and then follow these steps:

1. Select what to back up.

On the Backup tab, which is shown in Figure 2-16, click the check boxes next to the files, folders, disks, and other elements you want to back up.

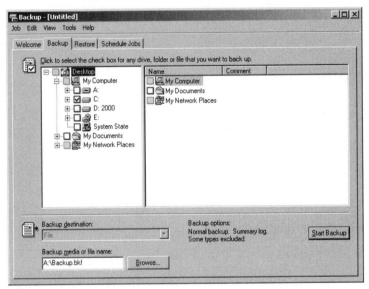

Figure 2-16 The Backup tab in the Backup window.

2. Select where to back up.

In the Backup Destination box, specify where to back up to.

3. Specify the name of the medium or the file.

In the Backup Media Or File Name box, enter or browse to the filename.

4. Verify your backup configuration settings.

Click the Tools menu, click Options to open the Options dialog box, as shown in Figure 2-17, and then click the General tab. If the options are to your liking, click OK.

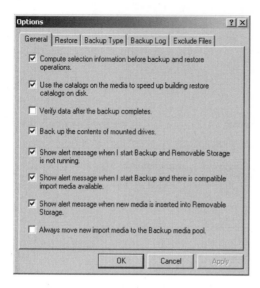

Figure 2-17 The General tab in the Options dialog box.

5. Start the backup.

On the Backup tab in the Backup window, click Start Backup.

You can exercise even more control over your backup by using the other tabs in the Options dialog box:

- Use the options on the Restore tab to specify what happens when duplicate files are found while you are restoring a backup.

- Use the options on the Backup Type tab to specify a backup type. Your choices are Normal (backs up all the selected files and clears the archive bit), Copy (backs up all selected files and does not clear the archive bit), Differential (backs up all files that have changed since the last Normal or Incremental back up and retains the archive bit for each file), Incremental (the same as Differential but clears the archive bit for each file), and Daily (backs up all files modified today).

NOTE *An archive bit indicates whether the file has been changed since it was last backed up.*

- Use the options on the Backup Log tab to specify whether and what type of information to store about the backup.

- Use the options on the Exclude Files tab to specify the file types you want to exclude from the backup.

On the Schedule Jobs tab in the Backup window, you can specify a date for the backup. The Schedule Jobs tab is shown in Figure 2-18.

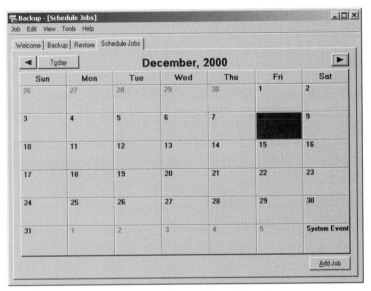

Figure 2-18 Selecting a date for the backup.

Backing up to a Web site

For still more protection, you can back up to a Web site, either instead of or as well as another medium. For starters, you might check with your ISP to see whether your Internet account includes storage space. Be sure to verify that others on the Internet won't be able to access your files. (Skill 6 talks in detail about using the Internet.)

Another possibility is backing up to a Web site that's been created for exactly that purpose. One option is *www.driveway.com*, which gives you free storage space just for signing up. If you are using any of the Microsoft Office suite of applications, you can save files to a Web folder on *driveway.com* just as easily as saving files to a local hard drive.

Restoring a backup with the wizard

Windows 2000 Professional has been described as crashless, and that is the case when you compare it with previous versions of Windows. When the inevitable happens, however, such as a hard disk crash, there's nothing that Windows 2000 can do. However, if you've been ruthlessly adhering to a backup schedule, you should be able to restore your lost information.

To restore files using the Restore Wizard, follow these steps:

1. **Start the Backup program.**

   Click the Start button, click Programs, click Accessories, click System Tools, and then click Backup.

2. **Start the Wizard.**

   On the Welcome tab, click the Restore Wizard button.

3. **Follow the onscreen instructions.**

   Specify what to restore, where to restore it from, the backup set to use, where to restore to, and how to restore, and then click the Start Restore button.

Restoring a backup manually

Restoring a backup manually involves essentially the same steps that the Restore Wizard walks you through, except that you use the Restore tab in the Backup window. Select the drive, folder, or file you want to restore, specify where to restore the backup, and click Start Restore to begin.

A word about viruses

A *virus* is a malevolent program that can attach itself to your computer system without your knowledge or permission and wipe out all your work in less than a minute. Computer viruses are not airborne; they travel via infected disks, e-mail, files you download from the Internet, and in rare instances, even in shrink-wrapped software. Many recent viruses replicate themselves by reading a recipient's address book and mailing themselves to all the people in it.

In addition to faithfully adhering to your backup schedule, what can you do to avoid falling prey to computer viruses? Here are some ideas:

- Acquire and use antivirus software regularly. In addition, keep it up-to-date. New viruses are being created all the time, and your antivirus software needs to know about them.

- Protect the integrity of your home computer or network and your office computer or network. It is common to catch a workplace virus and bring it home or to acquire a virus at home and then infect the office network.

- Never download a file or a software program if you don't know and trust the source.

- If an application supports it, turn on Macro Virus Protection. For example, in a Microsoft Office application, click the Tools menu, click Macro, click Security to open the Security dialog box, select High or Medium, and click OK.

- Don't believe everything you hear. There are as many *hoaxes* about viruses as there are viruses. To stay current, go to one of the antivirus software vendor's sites or check the Symantec AntiVirus Research Center's Web site at *www.symantec.com/avcenter/*.

Summary

This skill has given you lots of information you can use to organize and protect your files and folders. It looked at the types of files systems you can use with Windows 2000 Professional, how to work with Windows Explorer, how to set file and folder permissions, how to work with offline files, how to specify folder options, and how to back up and restore files and folders. Although acquiring these skills will make you more efficient in the workplace, if you take away only one thing from this skill, it should be how to use Windows Explorer. It is your primary tool for organizing your computer system.

PRINT WITH WINDOWS 2000 PROFESSIONAL

Featuring:

- Installing a Local Printer
- Printing Documents
- Managing the Printer
- Customizing the Printing Process
- Installing and Using Fonts

The vision of a paperless office is not a reality, and probably never will be, although the world seems to be getting closer with every passing year. The emergence of the Internet has contributed to the current state of affairs in a major way.

For example, five years ago, an author submitting something for publication typically copied the document file and the illustrations to a floppy disk, printed the text, printed the illustrations, and, because slow printers were common then, photocopied everything that was printed so that she or he could keep a reference copy. Then the printed copies and the floppy were sent to the publisher via an overnight delivery service. Now all the files are compressed and the publication is sent off as an attachment to e-mail. The author can keep a backup copy of the files on the network, and keep almost no paper files in the office.

In the meantime, printers have become cheaper and cheaper, are easier to use and maintain, and are substantially faster. Using some of the features that are available with Windows 2000 Professional or a small, rather inexpensive software package, you can print your own business cards, greetings cards, photographs, newsletters, and brochures, for example.

This skill looks at the steps to install and use a local printer with Windows 2000 Professional. A *local printer* is one that is physically attached to your computer by a cable. The next skill describes how to install a *network printer*, a printer that is attached to another computer on a network and is known as a *print server*.

Installing a Local Printer

If you upgraded to Windows 2000 Professional rather than performing a clean install on a new machine or a new partition on your hard drive, you might not have needed to install your printer. Windows 2000 Professional should have recognized it during installation in the same way as it recognized your keyboard and your monitor, for example. If you acquire a new printer, though, or if you do a clean install of Windows 2000 Professional, you'll need to install your printer. You do so by using the Add Printer Wizard, which you access from the Printers folder.

To install a local printer, follow these steps:

1. **Prepare the printer.**

    Be sure that the printer cable is securely connected to both the printer and your computer, follow any preparatory instructions that came with it, and turn on the printer. If your printer is a USB or Firewire printer, it will be automatically installed—follow any instructions provided, and you're finished.

2. **Open the Printers folder, which is shown in Figure 3-1.**

    Click the Start button, click Settings, and then click Printers.

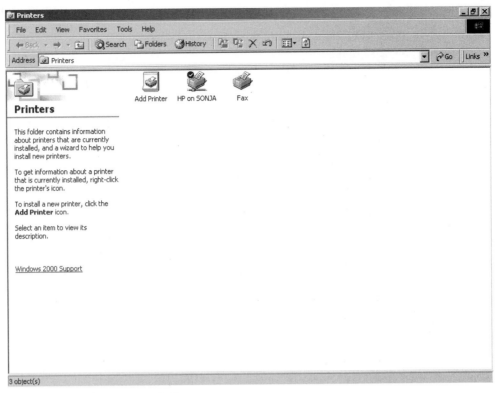

Figure 3-1   The Printers folder.

NOTE   *In Figure 3-1, I've already added a network printer and a fax printer to my system. If you don't have either and you haven't installed a local printer, you'll see only the Add Printer icon.*

3. Start the Add Printer Wizard.

Click the Add Printer icon to open the Welcome screen, as shown in Figure 3-2.

Figure 3-2   The Add Printer Wizard.

4. Specify a local printer.

Click Next, and click the Local Printer option button. If you have a new printer, it is probably Plug and Play, so also click the Automatically Detect And Install My Plug And Play Printer.

NOTE   *Plug and Play is a new feature in Windows 2000 Professional. If you've used Windows 95, Windows 98, or Windows Me, you probably know about Plug and Play, although it was not available in Windows NT. Before the advent of Plug and Play, you had to manually configure a new piece of hardware when you installed it in your computer, a process that took some technical knowledge and some time. Plug and Play does all this configuration for you, if the device you are installing is Plug and Play compatible.*

5. Specify the port to be used.

Click Next, and tell the wizard whether to use an existing port and which one or to create a new port. Normally, printers use LTP1, which is selected by default. Unless you have a good reason to do otherwise, accept the default port.

NOTE   *A printer port is the interface through which information between the computer and the printer passes, and is also referred to as the parallel port.*

6. **Specify the manufacturer and model of your printer.**

Click Next. On the Manufacturers list, select the manufacturer of your printer, and, on the Printers list, select the model.

7. **Name your printer.**

Click Next. In the Printer Name box, enter a name that will be associated with the icon for your printer in the Printers folder. If you want this printer to be used automatically when you print from a Windows application, click the Yes option button.

8. **Don't share your printer.**

Click Next. On this screen, you can specify whether to share your printer. Because this skill describes only how to install a local printer that is not connected to a network, click the Do Not Share This Printer option.

9. **Print a test page.**

Click Next. Printing a test page is always a good idea so that you can verify that your printer is up and running. Click the Yes option to display the summary screen of the Add Printer Wizard.

10. **Complete the wizard.**

On the summary screen, verify that all your printer settings are correct. If they are not, click the Back button to retrace your steps and change them. If the settings are correct, click Finish to complete the wizard and print your test page.

When you click Finish, Windows 2000 Professional copies the printer driver for your printer and you'll see an icon for this printer in the Printers folder.

NOTE   *A printer* driver *is a little program that lets a computer communicate with and control a printer. Windows 2000 Professional includes a number of printer drivers and probably found yours on the list automatically.*

Determining why your test page didn't print

If your test page didn't print or didn't print correctly, you are not out of luck. Here are some things you can do:

- In the dialog box that asks whether your test page printed correctly, click No. You'll see a list of troubleshooting steps. Work through them to see whether you can locate the problem (select an option, and then click Next). Figure 3-3 shows the first screen in the Print Troubleshooter, which you can also access through the Contents tab in Help.

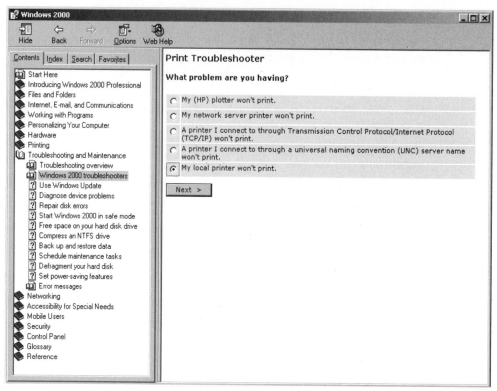

Figure 3-3   The Print Troubleshooter.

- If you work through the Troubleshooter and still can't print, make sure that your printer is on the Hardware Compatibility List (HCL) at *www.microsoft.com/hcl*.

- If your printer is not on the list, contact the manufacturer of your printer to see whether it has a driver compatible with Windows 2000 Professional. If you can't obtain a compatible driver, you most likely will need to acquire a printer that is compatible with Windows 2000 Professional. Again, check the HCL before you shop.

Removing a printer and other printer-related tasks

When you install a new printer and no longer need the driver for a previous printer, you can easily delete the driver. In the Printers folder, simply right-click the icon for the old printer, and choose Delete from the shortcut menu. Here are some other printer housekeeping tasks you'll need to do from time to time:

- To rename a printer, right-click its icon in the Printers folder, choose Rename from the shortcut menu, type a new name in the box, and then click outside the box.

- To set a different printer as the default, right-click the printer's icon in the Printers folder, and choose Set As Default Printer from the shortcut menu.

- To create a shortcut to a printer on the desktop, right-click the printer's icon in the Printers folder, choose Create Shortcut from the shortcut menu, and click Yes in the Shortcut dialog box. As the next section explains, you'll need a shortcut to your printer on the desktop if you want to use drag-and-drop to print.

Printing Documents

You can print from the desktop or from an application. In either case, Windows 2000 Professional is doing the printing. The print spooler program accepts the document and holds it on disk or in memory until the printer is free, and then the printer prints the document.

Printing from the desktop

You can print from the desktop using drag-and-drop, or you can right-click.

Using drag-and-drop

As mentioned in the preceding section, to print from the desktop using drag-and-drop, you need a shortcut to the printer, and you also need an open folder that contains the file you want to print. In other words, you need to be able to see both the printer icon and the filename or icon. Figure 3-4 shows someone in the process of using drag-and-drop to print. Follow these steps:

1. **Create a shortcut to your printer on the desktop.**

    See the preceding section for instructions.

2. **Open Windows Explorer.**

    Right-click My Computer and choose Explore from the shortcut menu. Navigate to the folder and then the file you want to print. Reposition the Windows Explorer window so that you can see both the printer icon and the file.

3. **Print the document.**

    Click the icon for the file, and drag it to the printer icon.

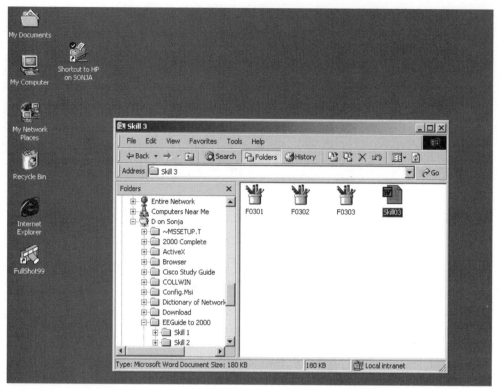

Figure 3-4   Printing with drag-and-drop.

The file opens in its associated application and then prints, using the default options in the Print dialog box, discussed later in this skill.

Using right-click

To print using the right-click method, follow these steps:

1. Locate the file.

In Windows Explorer, open a folder that contains the file you want to print.

2. Print the file.

Right-click the file's icon, and choose Print from the shortcut menu.

As is the case when you use drag-and-drop to print, the file opens in its associated application and prints using the default options in the Print dialog box.

Printing from within a Windows application

To easily and quickly print from an application, open the application, open the document, and click the Print toolbar button. Using the Print button, using drag-and-drop, and using the right-click method all print a document quickly, but, as mentioned, you pick up the default print settings when you use any of these methods. In other words, the entire file is printed, only one copy is printed, the printed output is portrait orientation (vertical), and the default paper size and paper tray are used.

To exercise finer control over how a document is printed, you need to print from an application. To print in WordPad, for example, follow these steps:

1. Open WordPad.

Click the Start button, click Programs, click Accessories, and then click WordPad.

2. Open a document.

Click the File menu, click Open to open the Open dialog box, select the file you want to print, and click Open.

3. Open the Print dialog box, as shown in Figure 3-5.

Click the File menu, and then click Print.

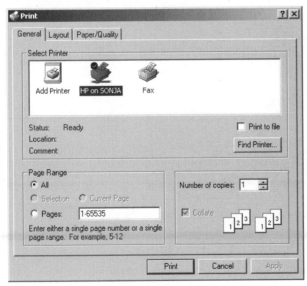

Figure 3-5   The Print dialog box.

4. Select a printer.

The printer you selected as a default is already selected. To select another printer, click it. Point at a printer to display its status in a ScreenTip.

5. Choose what to print.

In the Page Range area, choose whether to print the entire file, only a selection (what you selected before you opened the Print dialog box), or selected pages.

6. Specify the number of copies to print.

In the Number Of Copies spin box, select the number of copies you want to print. By default, multiple copies are collated. If you don't want them collated, clear the Collate check box.

7. Specify the orientation of the printed page.

Click the Layout tab, which is shown in Figure 3-6, and select Portrait to print vertically, or select Landscape to print horizontally.

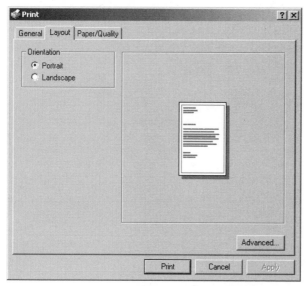

Figure 3-6 The Layout tab in the Print dialog box.

8. Set the paper source and quality of the print.

Click the Paper/Quality tab, which is shown in Figure 3-7.

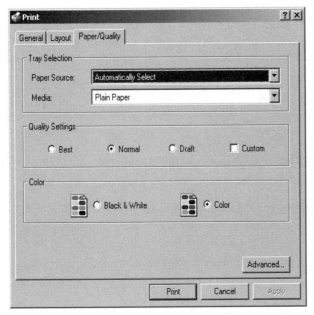

Figure 3-7   The Paper/Quality tab in the Print dialog box.

9. Print the document.

Click the Print button.

Printing to a file

When you print to a file, you don't send the document to your local printer or see any printed output. Instead, you save on disk the codes and data that are normally sent to the printer. This isn't something you necessarily do every day, but it's a handy thing to know about when you need it. You can even print to a file using a printer that isn't physically attached to your computer. To do so, simply install the printer you want to use and follow the steps earlier in this skill for installing a local printer.

To print to a file, follow these steps:

1. Install a printer.

If necessary, install an "imaginary" printer.

2. Open the Print dialog box.

In the application, click the File menu, and then click Print.

3. Choose a printer.

On the General tab in the Print dialog box, select a printer.

4. Print the document to a file.

Click the Print To File check box, click Print to open the Print To File dialog box, as shown in Figure 3-8, enter a name for the file, and click OK. The file is stored in your My Documents folder.

Figure 3-8   The Print To File dialog box.

To later print this document on a real printer click the Start button, click Programs, click Accessories, and then click Command Prompt. At the command prompt, type the following line (assuming you want to print to your parallel port and the print file is document.prn on a floppy disk):

print /lpt1 a:\document.prn

Managing the Printer

After you click Print, your document wends its way through the printing process. What if you suddenly realize, though, that you've sent the wrong document to the printer and it's more than 100 pages? You can reach over and turn off the printer, but that's not the best solution, and sometimes the printer isn't close at hand. The best way to manage the printer is to use the window that opens when you double-click the printer's icon in the Printers folder. The printer window is shown in Figure 3-9.

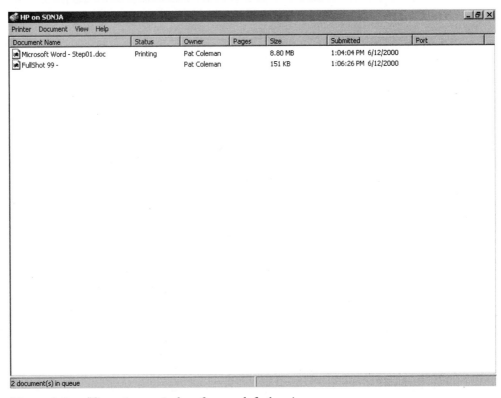

Figure 3-9   The printer window for my default printer.

Here's a description of what each column in the printer window displays:

- The Document Name column displays the name of the document and its associated application.

- The Status column indicates whether the document is being printed, paused, or deleted.

- The Owner column displays the name of the person who sent the document to the printer.

- The Pages column indicates the number of pages currently printed.

- The Size column displays the size of the document in bytes.

- The Submitted column displays the time and the date the document was sent to the printer.

- The Port column reports the port being used.

Use the following techniques to manage a printer in the printer's window:

- To cancel the printing of a document, right-click it, and choose Cancel from the shortcut menu.

- To cancel the printing of all documents in the print queue, click the Printer menu, and then click Cancel All Documents.

- To temporarily halt the printing of a document, right-click it, and choose Pause from the shortcut menu.

- To resume printing a document, right-click it, and choose Resume from the shortcut menu.

You'll notice that printing doesn't cease the second you choose Pause or Cancel. Whatever pages have already been spooled to the printer's buffer must print before the printing is halted.

Customizing the Printing Process

To specify such settings as the paper source for a printer and the print quality, you use the printer's Properties dialog box. Before finding out how to use this dialog box, though, you need to understand about properties in Windows 2000 Professional.

In Windows 2000 Professional, every component is an *object*. For example, your hard drive is an object, My Network Places is an object, your keyboard is an object, your printer is an object, and a document is an object. And all objects have *properties*, or settings that determine how the object looks and works. To configure an object, you can use its Properties dialog box. Thus, to specify the settings for a printer, you use the printer's Properties dialog box.

To open a printer's Properties dialog box, follow these steps:

1. **Open the Printers folder.**

   Click the Start button, click Settings, and then click Printers.

2. **Open a printer's Properties dialog box.**

   Right-click a printer's icon, and choose Properties from the shortcut menu.

Figure 3-10 shows the Properties dialog box for an HP DeskJet. As you can see, it has eight tabs. The number of tabs and the options within each depend on the printer. The DeskJet can print in color and in black and white, so its Properties dialog box contains a Color Management tab. The printer is also on a network, so the dialog box has a Sharing tab. Depending on your printer and its capabilities, you might have more or fewer tabs.

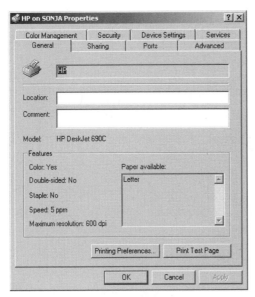

Figure 3-10 The Properties dialog box for a printer.

Look at the options you can use on the tabs in the printer's Properties dialog box to customize your printer so that it's appropriate for your environment. The settings you establish in a printer's Properties dialog box become the default for that printer.

Using the General tab

On the face of the General tab, you can change only a couple of settings—Location and Comment. Both are typically used for printers on a network, and they are described in the next skill.

To specify orientation, click the Printing Preferences button to open the Printing Preferences dialog box for your printer. It has the same Layout and Paper/Quality tabs as the Print dialog box discussed earlier in this skill.

In the Printing Preference dialog box, click the Advanced tab to open the Advanced Options dialog box, which is shown in Figure 3-11. You use the options in this dialog box to specify the default paper size, copy count, and print quality of graphics, for example. When you click an underlined option, you'll see a drop-down list box from which you can make selections.

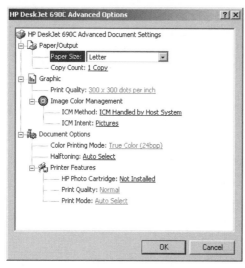

Figure 3-11 The Advanced Options dialog box for a printer.

Using the Sharing tab

You use the Sharing tab if your printer is on a network. The following skill looks at the options on this tab.

Using the Ports tab

You use the settings on the Ports tab, which is shown in Figure 3-12, to add, delete, and configure ports. (In Figure 3-12, some options are grayed out because the example doesn't show a local printer connected to a Windows 2000 Professional computer. The printer that is used on the network is connected to another computer.) Most people never need to experiment with the settings on this tab, but in case your printer port ever accidentally gets deleted, you need to know how to add it back. Follow these steps:

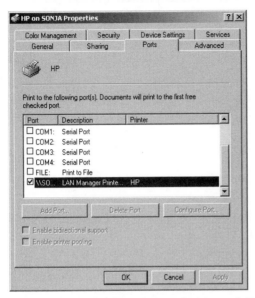

Figure 3-12 The Ports tab in the printer's Properties dialog box.

1. Open the Printer Ports dialog box.

Click the Add Port button.

2. Add a local port.

Click the New Port button, enter a name for the port (such as LPT1), and click OK.

3. Close the Printer Ports dialog box.

Click the Close button to return to the Ports tab. The new port will appear on the list.

Using the Advanced tab

You use the options on the Advanced tab, which is shown in Figure 3-13, to specify a number of settings:

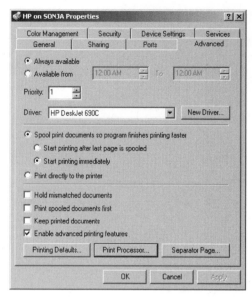

Figure 3-13   The Advanced tab in the printer's Properties dialog box.

- The priority of the printing document (1 is the highest; 99 is the lowest).

- A new printer driver.

- Whether documents will be spooled or sent directly to the printer.

- Whether mismatched documents will be held. (*Mismatched* documents are those whose setup doesn't match the printer setup.)

- Whether documents will be stored in the print queue.

By default, documents are spooled and start printing immediately, and the Enable Advanced Printing Features check box is checked. Which features are enabled depends on the features available with your printer.

If you are having problems with your printer and think that they might be related to your printer driver, you might be able to download a newer printer driver from the manufacturer's Web site or obtain a driver on disk from the manufacturer. In either case, click the New Driver button to start the Add Printer Driver Wizard and install the new driver.

Clicking the Printing Defaults button opens the Printing Defaults dialog box, which contains the same Layout and Paper/Quality tabs you saw earlier, in the Print dialog box. Clicking the Print Processor button opens the Print Processor dialog box, which lists the available print processors and the default data types. Don't mess with the options in this dialog box unless you are told by an informed technician to do so.

Using the Services tab

The Services tab for a sample printer is shown in Figure 3-14. Whether you have such a tab and which options are on it depend on your printer. As you can see, buttons can be clicked to align or clean the print cartridges.

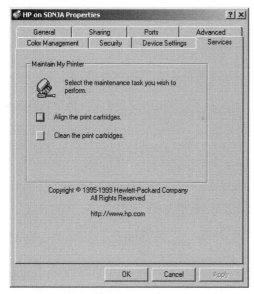

Figure 3-14 The Services tab in the printer's Properties dialog box.

Using the Device Settings tab

If you have more than one paper tray on your printer, click the Device Settings tab, which is shown in Figure 3-15, to specify which size paper is printed from which tray. You can select a tray in the Print dialog box when you print from an application.

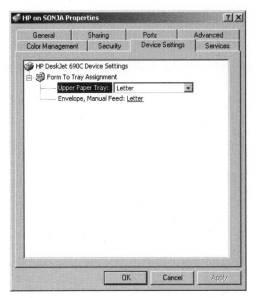

Figure 3-15   The Device Settings tab in the printer's Properties dialog box.

Using the Security tab

You use this tab primarily if you are sharing your computer with others on a network, although you can also use these settings if multiple people use one Windows 2000 Professional computer and you have user profiles set up. Skill 4 looks at printer security on a network.

Using the Color Management tab

A printer that can print in color has a Color Management tab, as shown in Figure 3-16. The settings on this tab associate color profiles with your printer. A color profile contains information about color, hue, saturation, and brightness. When you install a scanner, a monitor, or a printer, Windows 2000 Professional automatically installs a color profile that is appropriate for the device. For most uses, this profile is sufficient and is selected by default.

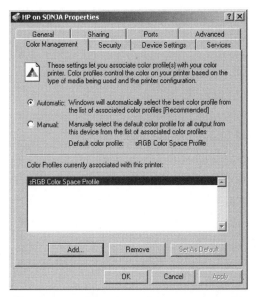

Figure 3-16 The Color Management tab in the printer's Properties dialog box.

If you are a graphics artist or if you produce complex color publications, you might want to install another color profile that lets you better control how colors are printed on your printer. To do so, follow these steps:

1. **Open the Add Profile Association dialog box, which is shown in Figure 3-17.**

   Click the Add button.

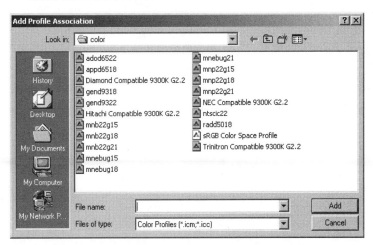

Figure 3-17 The Add Profile Association tab in the printer Properties dialog box.

2. Select a new profile.

Click a color profile from the list, and then click Add. On the Color Management tab, click OK.

To delete a color profile, select it on the Color Management tab, and click Remove.

Installing and Using Fonts

When you print using any of the methods described in this skill, you use a particular typeface, or *font*. Examples of fonts included with Windows 2000 Professional are Comic Sans MS (a popular font for use on Web pages), Courier (which looks like a typewriter did the printing), and Times New Roman (the default selection for printing in Windows applications). To see the entire selection of fonts, follow these steps:

1. Open Control Panel.

Click the Start button, click Settings, and then click Control Panel.

2. Open the Fonts folder, which is shown in Figure 3-18.

Click the Fonts icon.

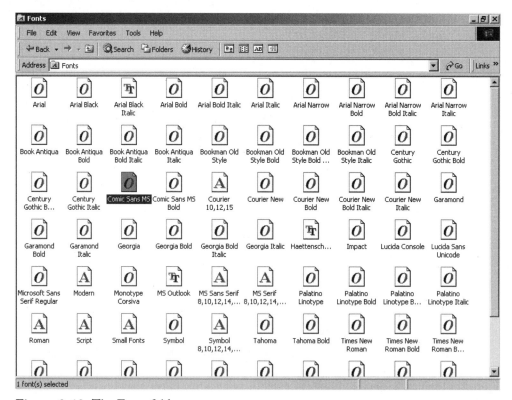

Figure 3-18 The Fonts folder.

Notice that fonts are identified with a lettered icon, which indicates the type of font it is. Windows 2000 Professional provides four types of fonts:

- The icon containing the double-letter *T* indicates a TrueType font. The printed output of a TrueType font is identical to what you see on the screen.

- The icon containing the letter *O* indicates an OpenType font, which is an extension of TrueType. An OpenType font also looks the same on the screen and when it is printed, and it can be rotated and scaled to various sizes.

- The icon containing the letter *A* indicates either a vector font or raster font. *Vector* fonts are used primarily with plotters; the three vector fonts included with Windows 2000 Professional are Modern, Roman, and Script. *Raster* fonts are stored as bitmap images. These fonts cannot be scaled or rotated and won't print if your printer doesn't support them. The raster fonts included with Windows 2000 Professional are Courier, MS SansSerif, MS Serif, Small, and Symbol.

A font can have size, which is measured in points (1 point is 1/72 inch) and style (for example, italics or boldface). To see what a particular font looks like in various sizes, double-click its icon. Figure 3-19 shows how Comic Sans MS looks in various sizes. To print this screen, click the Print button.

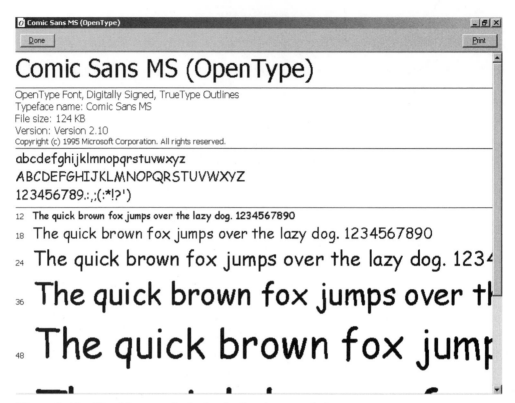

Figure 3-19 Checking out the look of a font in several sizes.

To display a list of fonts that are similar, click the View menu, click List Fonts By Similarity, and select a font from the drop-down list. To display only basic fonts and not all variations, such as roman, italic, bold, and bold italic, for example, click the View menu, and then click Hide Variations.

Changing the font in an application

To change the default font and print a document in a font you specify, you must print from an application. The steps are the same in most Windows applications. Follow these steps to specify the font for a printed document in WordPad:

1. **Open WordPad.**

   Click the Start button, click Programs, click Accessories, and then click WordPad.

2. **Open the Font dialog box, which is shown in Figure 3-20.**

   Click the Format menu, and then click Font.

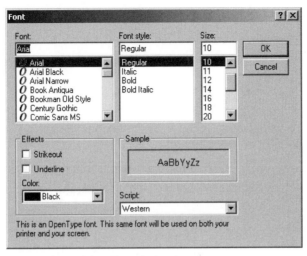

Figure 3-20 The Font dialog box.

3. Select a different font.

Select a font, a font style, a size, a color, and an effect, and then click OK.

Installing a new font

Although Windows 2000 Professional comes with a great many fonts in all sorts of styles and sizes, you might want to install other fonts for particular purposes. Follow these steps to do so:

1. Open the Add Fonts dialog box, which is shown in Figure 3-21.

In the Fonts folder, click the File menu, and then click Install New Font.

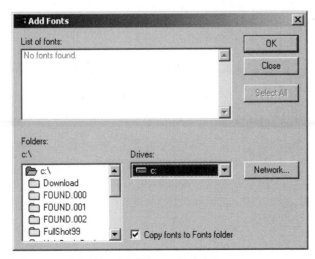

Figure 3-21 The Add Fonts dialog box.

2. Locate and install the font.

On the Drives drop-down list, select the drive where the font is stored, and click OK. By default, fonts are copied to the Fonts folder.

Summary

This skill looked at how to install a local printer, at the various ways to print in Windows 2000 Professional, at how to manage the printing process, at how to customize the way your printer works, and at how to use and install fonts. You'll find all the information concerning network printers—how to install, share, and use them—in the next skill.

Skill 4

WORK ON A NETWORK

Featuring:

- Setting Up a Small Network
- Installing and Using a Network Printer
- Setting Up Users and Groups
- Installing Applications
- Network Tips and Tricks
- Connecting to a Corporate Network

Corporate computer networks have been around for a long time. I first worked on one in the early 1980s at *Encyclopaedia Britannica*, where each user clicked away at a 3270 terminal connected to the mainframe that sat in its sacred air-conditioned room on an upper floor. On the mainframe resided all the articles that comprised the mother of all encyclopedias, and, with the proper rights and permissions, you could access and edit those articles. To do other things, such as develop a departmental budget or compose and print a memo, 250 people shared a lone PC.

The networking world has come a long way. These days home networks are not uncommon, most small businesses are networked, and you would be hard-pressed to find in a corporation a lone PC that's not connected to a network of some type and to the Internet. Although the Windows 2000 family of operating systems was developed primarily for the corporate world, as you will see in this skill, you can easily use Windows 2000 Professional to set up a simple network in a small- to medium-size office or to set up a network in your home office.

How do you know whether a network could benefit your business? Well, take a look at some of the things you can do even on a small network:

- Share files, folders, and applications.

- Share a printer and other devices.

- Share an Internet connection.

- Back up to another computer.

- Create an e-business and run it off your network.

- Run multiplayer games.

- Access your corporate network from home and vice versa.

- With Windows 2000 Professional, secure your system and, therefore, your data.

This list is far from exhaustive.

After looking at how to set up, configure, and use a simple network, this skill gives you some tips about working on a corporate network.

Setting Up a Small Network

If you glance again at the preceding list, you'll see that the operative word is *sharing*. The real purpose of a network is to share resources. You don't need a printer for every computer in your office; you can set up one printer that everyone can share. Setting up a network can be cost effective as well as a productivity tool.

Before getting into the how-to-do-it part, though, you have to understand a little about network structure and design. Just as you need to understand about the file systems you can use with Windows 2000 Professional before you install the operating system, you need to understand network structure and design so that you can set up a network that meets your specific needs. After all, that's why you're thinking about a network in the first place—so that your business operations run more efficiently and, in the long run, so that your business is more profitable.

Understanding the network types

This section and the next use some technical terms you might not be familiar with. Don't tune out. One of my colleagues describes the skill level needed to set up a network as about the same as making a pot of coffee. I don't know about that comparison, but it's certainly easier than programming a VCR!

One of your first decisions is about network type, and you have two choices: peer-to-peer and client/server. In a *peer-to-peer network,* all computers are equals. Each computer has its own hard drive and can see and talk to all the other computers on the network. In addition, each computer can share its resources, such as a CD-ROM drive, a printer, files, folders, and applications, for example.

On a *client/server network,* one or more computers stores resources and supplies (*serves*) them to the other computers. All the other computers are connected to this central computer (or computers), which manages applications, files, or printers, for example. Corporate networks are generally client/server networks and are managed by a system administrator.

In this skill, you set up a peer-to-peer network, which is ideal for a small business or a home office.

Designing your network

After you decide on a network type, you need to decide how your network will be designed physically. The technical term for physical design is *topology,* and you can choose from three basic types:

- Star, in which all the computers are connected to a central hub like the points of a star. A star topology typically uses 10BaseT or 100BaseT cabling. (The following section describes this type of cabling.)

- Bus, in which all the computers are connected to a single cable. The bus topology uses coaxial cable.

- Ring, in which all the computers are connected via a closed circle of cabling. The topology is not in common use.

Technology experts often discuss topologies and which physical design actually corresponds to a theoretical topology. This skill uses the star design, the one that's best suited to a peer-to-peer network. In this skill, you connect each computer on the network to a central hub.

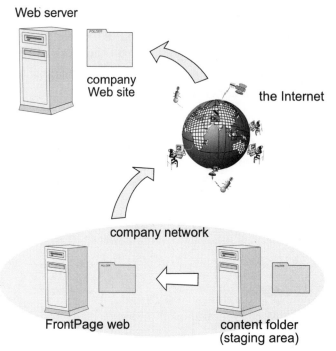

Web server

company
Web site

the Internet

company network

FrontPage web

content folder
(staging area)

Figure 4-1   A small network.

Obtaining what you need

A couple of network components have been mentioned that now need explanation: cable and a hub. Cabling and a hub are only two of the necessary components, though; you also need network interface cards (NICs). The following list describes what each item does:

- *100BaseT cabling* is the physical connection between the computers on the network and the hub. While you *can* get two grades of cable—Category 3 UTP and Category 5 UTP (UTP is short for unshielded twisted-pair)—Category 5 cabling has all but completely replaced Category 3 cabling because it permits 100 Mbps operation, while Category 3 is limited to 10Mbps. The cable length you can use with 10Mbps networks runs from a minimum of 8 feet to a maximum of 328 feet. The maximum length for a 100Mbps network using UTP cabling is 165 feet.

- A *hub* is the central device that connects all the computers on the network. The hub itself doesn't require any software or configuration; it is simply the device that allows all the computers to communicate. The number of connections on the hub (the number of places to which you can connect a cable that is connected to a computer on the other end) determines the number of computers that can be on the network. Be sure to buy a hub that has enough connections for the number of computers you want to connect, and that is the right speed for your network (10Mbps, 100Mbps, or a switching hub that supports both). Also, if you plan on expanding your network to add more computers or you anticipate using an ISDN, DSL, or cable modem connection, make sure that the hub contains an uplink port.

- A *network interface card* goes into each computer on the network and connects to one of the slots on the computer's motherboard. (The *motherboard* is the main printed circuit board in a computer.) The slots on the motherboard can be one of two types: Industry Standard Architecture (ISA) and Peripheral Component Interconnect (PCI). A NIC will work with one type or the other, but not with both. Most newer computers have PCI slots, but you'll need to find out which type your computer uses. (I strongly recommend using PCI network cards—they're faster and easier to install.) When purchasing a NIC, make sure to get one that supports 100Mbps operation, even if you choose to use a 10Mbps network, since the card supports both speeds and this allows you to easily upgrade as your needs grow. Also make sure to check the Windows 2000 Hardware Compatibility List (HCL) at *www.microsoft.com/hcl* before purchasing a NIC.

NOTE   *If you have a laptop, you'll probably either have a network card built into your computer (look for a somewhat larger than usual phone jack on your laptop), or you'll have to buy a PC card network adapter (also known as PCMCIA card).*

You can shop for these parts and pieces at your local computer store or on the Internet. Another option is to buy a starter kit that contains everything you need to connect a couple of computers for less than $100. This is often a great way to get started, and if you need to connect additional computers, simply buy extra NICs and cabling.

Connecting your network

After deciding on the physical layout of your system, gathering all the pieces in one place, and assembling your starter kit or your components, get yourself a screwdriver, and follow these steps:

1. **Insert the NIC into each computer.**

   Turn off all computers and peripherals, and unplug them. Open the case, and insert the NIC in an empty slot, according to the manufacturer's instructions. Be sure that the card bracket is sitting snugly in the case. Replace the case.

2. **Connect the cables.**

   Connect one end of the cable to the NIC, and connect the other end of the cable to the hub, starting with the first connection. Do this for each computer on the network, and then plug the hub into the power source. By the way, both ends of the cable are identical, so it doesn't make any difference which end you connect to the computer or the hub.

3. **Power up the system.**

   Turn on the hub and all connected computers. You should see a light on the hub for each connected computer.

That's all there is to it. The first time you do this procedure, it might take you awhile, especially if you've never taken the lid off your computer. But the next NIC you insert will take you half that time, and soon you'll be inserting NICs confidently and easily. Now you're ready to install and configure your network.

Configuring your network

To configure your network, you have to give Windows 2000 Professional some information about the network you've just set up. When you power up your system, the Windows 2000 Professional Plug-and-Play system loads the device drivers you need for the NICs. Your next order of business is to specify the network protocols you will use. A protocol specifies the rules that will be used when you transmit and receive data over a network. The protocol that is best suited for our small network is NetBIOS Extended User Interface (NetBEUI), although any network that desires Internet access will also need to run TCP/IP.

To configure your network, follow these steps:

1. **Open the Network And Dial-Up Connections window, as shown in Figure 4-2.**

   Log on as an administrator, right-click My Network Places on the desktop, and choose Properties from the shortcut menu.

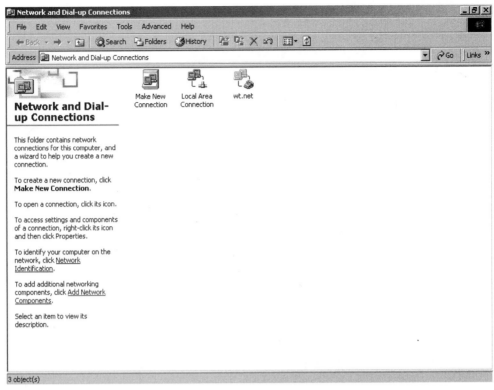

Figure 4-2   The Network And Dial-Up Connections window.

2. Open the Local Area Connection Properties dialog box, as shown in Figure 4-3.

Right-click Local Area Connection, and choose Properties from the shortcut menu.

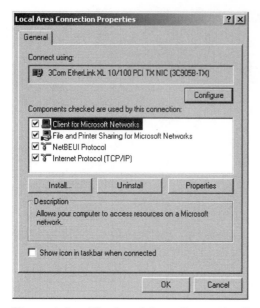

Figure 4-3   The Local Area Connection Properties dialog box.

3. Check to see which protocols are installed.

The list in the Local Area Connection Properties dialog box should contain at least these protocols:

- Client For Microsoft Networks

- File And Printer Sharing For Microsoft Networks

- NetBEUI Protocol

TIP   *Any computers that need to access the Internet will also need to be running the TCP/IP protocol. While TCP/IP can be difficult to configure, on small networks Windows 2000 can autoconfigure TCP/IP for you, allowing your computers to easily communicate with each other.*

The list might also contain other protocols, and that's okay, but it must contain these three.

4. Add any needed protocols.

Click Install to open the Select Network Component Type dialog box, as shown in Figure 4-4. To install a component, select it, and click Add. When all components are added, click OK.

Figure 4-4   The Select Network Component Type dialog box.

5. Close the Local Area Connection Properties dialog box.

Click OK, and then click OK again when you are asked to restart the computer.

To see whether everything is in working order, follow these steps after you restart your computer:

1. Open the Computer Management window, which is shown in Figure 4-5.

Click the Start button, click Settings, click Control Panel to open Control Panel, click Administrative Tools, and then click Computer Management.

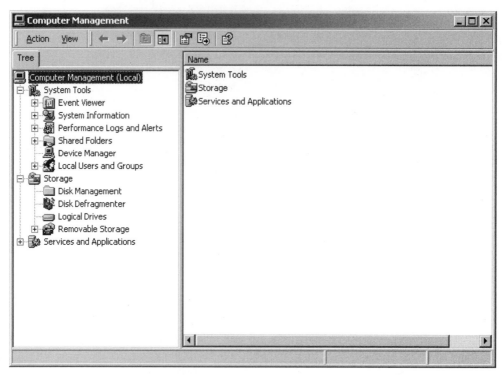

Figure 4-5 The Computer Management window.

2. Display a list of the devices installed on your computer.

In the Tree pane, click System Tools to expand it (if necessary), and then click Device Manager to display a list of the devices installed on your computer in the right pane. You'll see something similar to the list shown in Figure 4-6.

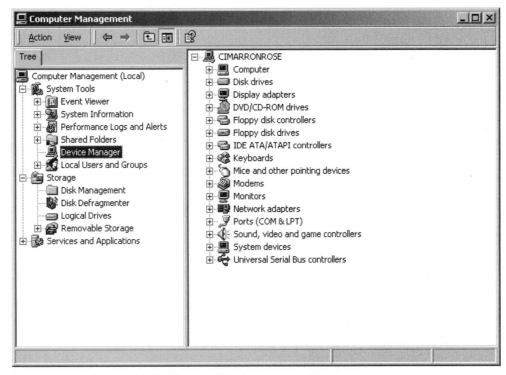

Figure 4-6   A list of the devices installed on my computer.

3. Expand Network Adapters.

Click the plus sign next to Network Adapters. If you don't see a yellow exclamation point or a red arrow next to the icon for your adapter, everything is working just as it's supposed to work.

Sharing resources with the network

Before users on your network can share resources—drives, files, folders, and applications, for example—the resources must be shared. On a peer-to-peer network, therefore, the user at each workstation must specifically mark their resources as shared. Sometimes these shared resources are simply called *shares*.

To set up a share, follow these steps:

1. Open Windows Explorer.

Right-click the My Computer icon and choose Explore from the shortcut menu.

2. Open the Properties dialog box for the resource you want to share.

Navigate to the resource you want to share, right-click it, and choose Sharing from the shortcut menu. You'll open a Properties dialog box at the Sharing tab and see something similar to what is shown in Figure 4-7.

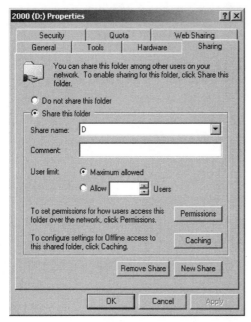

Figure 4-7   The Sharing tab in the Properties dialog box.

3. Share and name the resource.

First, click the Share This Folder option button. Then, in the Share Name box, you can accept the name that Windows 2000 Professional suggests or enter another name. This name must be unique on this computer, and it is the name that others on the network will see when they browse this computer. Give some thought to how you name resources. For example, you can certainly name a drive on your computer as D, but naming it something like StevesDriveD is much more descriptive and helpful when users browse the network.

4. Enter a comment.

In the Comment box, you can briefly describe the share. Users will also see this information when they are browsing the network.

5. **Specify the maximum number of users who can access this shared resource simultaneously.**

In the User Limit area, click Maximum Allowed or click Allow and then specify the maximum number of simultaneous users. The maximum that Windows 2000 Professional allows is 10 users. If the 11th person tries to log on, they will see this message: No more connections can be made to this remote computer at this time because there are already as many connections as the computer allows.

6. **Set the permissions for this resource.**

Click the Permissions button to open the Permissions dialog box for this share. You'll see something similar to Figure 4-8, depending on the resource you are sharing. For information on the types of permissions and how to set them, look back at Skill 2. Remember that you can set permissions on files and folders only if you are using the NTFS file system.

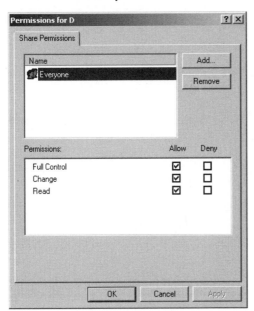

Figure 4-8   Setting permissions.

7. **Set caching options.**

Offline Files, as discussed in Skill 2, stores a version of shared network files on the hard drive in an area called the *cache*. Your computer can access these files even if you are not connected to the network. To specify how files are cached, click the Caching button to open the Caching Settings dialog box, as shown in Figure 4-9. You allow or disallow caching of the shared resource, and you choose from Manual Caching For Documents, Automatic Caching For Documents, and Automatic Caching For Programs. Select a setting, and then click OK.

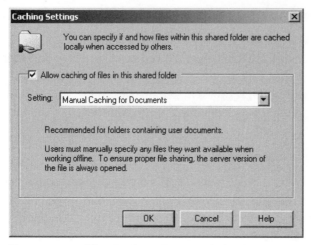

Figure 4-9   The Caching Settings dialog box.

8. Close the Properties dialog box.

Click OK.

Shared resources are identified in Windows Explorer with a hand under the icon for the resource.

If you change your mind and decide that you don't want to share a resource you have already shared, follow the steps above to open the Sharing tab, click the Remove Share button, and then click OK.

Accessing network resources

To access shared resources on your network, follow these steps:

1. Open My Network Places.

Double-click My Network Places on the desktop, or navigate to My Network Places in Windows Explorer.

2. Navigate to the resource.

Click the icon for the computer you want to use, and then browse until you locate the file, folder, and application, for example.

Mapping network drives

If you frequently use a particular network resource, you can map a network drive to it in order to access it quickly. That resource then appears as though it were a drive on your own computer. Suppose that you are working on a long document stored in a folder on another computer on your network. Follow these steps to map a drive to it:

1. Open the Map Network Drive dialog box, which is shown in Figure 4-10.

Right-click My Network Places on the desktop, and choose Map Network Drive from the shortcut menu.

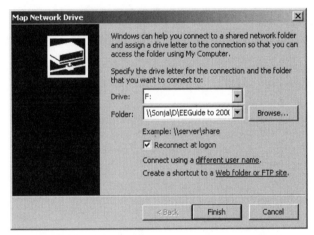

Figure 4-10   The Map Network Drive dialog box.

2. Specify the drive letter.

In the Drive drop-down list box, click the down arrow and select an unused letter. The default is the next drive in sequence. For example, in Figure 4-10, the default is F. The letters *C, D,* and *E* are already being used for existing drives on this computer.

3. Locate the file you want to map.

In the Folder drop-down list box, enter the path to the file or click Browse to locate it. If you want to reconnect to this file the next time you log on, click the Reconnect At Logon check box. Click Finish.

Opening a specific file on another computer is now as easy as opening a file on your local computer. You no longer have to browse My Network Places to find it.

If you no longer need access to a mapped drive, open My Computer, right-click the drive, and choose Disconnect from the shortcut menu. You can always remap to the drive if you need to do so. Nothing happens to it when you disconnect—the resource is still right where it was to begin with.

Installing and Using a Network Printer

One of the most common reasons for setting up a network is to share a printer. You can physically connect a printer to your network in a couple of ways:

- If your printer has a NIC in it, you can connect it directly to your hub.

- If your printer does have a NIC in it, connect the printer to a computer on the network.

Before you can install a network printer, you must do the following:

- Get the network up and running.

- Connect the printer to the network.

- Turn on the printer.

- Install the printer on a computer on the network.

- Share the printer.

After you turn on your printer and connect it directly to the network, use the following steps to complete setting up your network printer:

1. Open the Printers folder, which is shown in Figure 4-11.

Click the Start button, click Settings, and then click Printers.

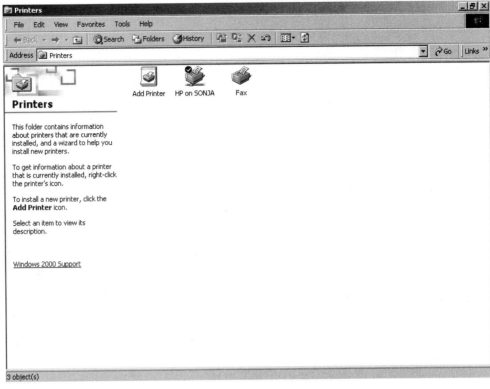

Figure 4-11 The Printers folder.

2. Start the Add Printer Wizard, as shown in Figure 4-12.

Click the Add Printer icon.

Figure 4-12 The Add Printer Wizard

3. Select to install a network printer.

At the Welcome screen, click Next. On the next screen, select the Network Printer option, and click Next.

4. Specify the name of the network printer.

Enter the name of the network printer. If you don't know the name, click Next to open a screen that displays the available resources on your network. Find the printer, select it, and then click Next.

5. Specify whether this printer is the default printer.

Click Yes if you want this printer set as the default. (You can always change the default printer by right-clicking the printer's icon in the Printers folder and choosing Set As Default Printer from the shortcut menu.) Click Next.

6. Copy the printer drivers to finish installing the network printer.

Click Finish to copy the drivers and print a test page. If the test page doesn't print successfully, follow the steps in the Print Troubleshooter, described in Skill 3.

To remove a network printer, to rename it, or to create a shortcut to it on the desktop, right-click its icon in the Printers folder, and choose the appropriate command from the shortcut menu. For details, see Skill 3.

Sharing a network printer

If you've already installed a local printer on your computer and you want to set it up as a shared printer on the network, follow these steps:

1. **Open the Properties dialog box for your printer.**

   In the Printers folder, right-click the icon for your printer, and choose Sharing from the shortcut menu to open the Properties dialog box for your printer on the Sharing tab, as shown in Figure 4-13.

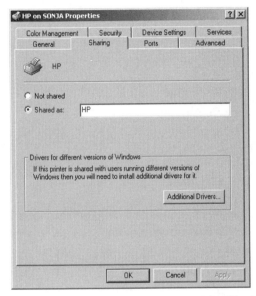

Figure 4-13   Using the options on the Sharing tab to share a printer.

2. **Share and name this printer.**

   Accept the name that is generated, or enter a new name. Click the General tab if you want to enter a description of this printer in the Comment field. I sometimes use this field to describe the printer's location, such as in Room 321 on the third floor. Click OK when you are finished.

You'll see a hand under the icon for this printer in the Printers folder, indicating that this is a shared printer.

Setting printer permissions

When you install and set up a network printer, that printer is available to everyone on the network. If you want, you can set limits on who can access and manage a printer. You can specify these permissions:

- Print is assigned to everyone by default and lets everyone print to the printer.

- Manage Printers lets a user pause or restart the printer, share the printer, and change the properties and the permissions.

- Manage Documents lets a user pause resume, restart, or cancel print jobs submitted by other users but prevents the user herself from printing documents on the printer.

To set up printer permissions, follow these steps:

1. Open the Properties dialog box for the shared printer.

Click the Start button, click Settings, and then click Printers to open the Printers folder. Right-click the icon for the shared printer, and choose Properties.

2. Set the permissions.

Click the Security tab. Select a user from the Name list, and then click the check box that corresponds with the permission you want that user to have. To add a group whose name does not appear on the Name list, click Add to open the Select Users, Computer, or Groups dialog box. Select a group, click Add, and then click OK. Back on the Security tab, select that group's name from the list, and check the permissions you want the group members to have. When you're done, click OK.

Using a network printer

You use a network printer just as you use a local printer. For all the details, see Skill 3.

Setting up separator pages

A handy device to use for a network printer is a separator page. A *separator page* prints between each print job, making it easier for users to identify their particular documents. To set up a separator page, follow these steps:

1. Open the printer's Properties dialog box.

Click the Start button, click Settings, and then click Printers to open the Printers folder. Right-click the network printer, and choose Properties from the shortcut menu.

2. **Open the Separator Page dialog box, which is shown in Figure 4-14.**

Click the Advanced tab in the Properties dialog box, and then click the Separator Page button.

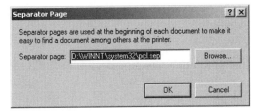

Figure 4-14   Creating a separator page.

3. **Select a separator page to use.**

In the Separator Page box, enter a filename for a separator page, or click Browse to locate one. Several separator page files are stored in the System32 folder. Click OK after you've selected a page.

Setting Up Users and Groups

Because Windows 2000 Professional is a secure operating system, you must set up a user account on a system before you can do anything. As you might remember, when you installed Windows 2000 Professional, you set up the Administrator account, and you may have set up a separate user account for yourself. The user account is an integral part of Windows 2000 Professional and has some great benefits, both on a standalone computer that is used by more than one person and on a network.

For example, if you and another person share a computer—maybe one works the early shift and the other works the late shift—you can set things up so that accessing each other's data is impossible unless you specifically give that person permission.

Understanding user and group accounts

The two broad categories of accounts in Windows 2000 Professional are users and groups. A *user* account identifies a user by his or her username and password. A *group* account contains other accounts that share common privileges.

User accounts are of three types:

- Normal allows a user to log on locally, shut down the system, create files, and delete files. A normal user might also have additional rights that an administrator assigns to him or her.

- Administrator gives the person full and complete rights to the computer, which means that an administrator can do just about anything to the computer. You cannot delete the Administrator account, and you must log on as Administrator when you need to create accounts or install software, for example.

- Guest lets a user log on to the computer even if he does not have an account on the system. This account presents a security risk. By default, it is disabled, and you should leave it that way. If a user needs access to the system and doesn't have an account, create one; don't use the guest account.

WARNING *You may want to avoid staying logged on as Administrator just because you can. Because you are all powerful, you can accidentally do something to damage your system that makes it necessary to completely reinstall Windows 2000 Professional. Create a user account for yourself, and use it until you need to do something that requires the rights of Administrator. However, if security isn't an issue for you and it's too much of an inconvenience to log on as an Administrator (or hold down the Shift key, right-click on a program, and choose Run As from the shortcut menu to logon as the Administrator) every time you want to maintain your system, then give your user account Administrator privileges.*

By default, Windows 2000 Professional contains a set of group accounts, although you can create other groups, as you'll see later in this section. Here is a list of the default groups and what each one can do:

- Administrators can do just about anything to the computer, including loading and unloading device drivers, installing software, setting up an audit, and taking ownership of objects.

- Backup Operators can log on to the system, back up and restore the system or selected files, and shut down the system.

- Guests have limited access to the system, and, as mentioned earlier in this skill, these accounts should not be used.

- Power Users can share files and printers, change the system time, force a shutdown of the system, and change the priorities of system processes.

- Replicators are involved in processes that involve a system connected to a Windows 2000 Server, so I won't get into that here.

- Users can run programs, access data, shut down a computer, and access data over the network.

Understanding user rights

In Windows 2000 Professional, the ability to perform a certain function is a user *right*. User rights are an important aspect of security. To see a list of user rights and to whom they are typically assigned, follow these steps:

1. **Open Control Panel.**

   Click the Start button, click Settings, and then click Control Panel.

2. **Open the Local Security Settings window, which is shown in Figure 4-15.**

   In Control Panel, click Administrative Tools, and then click Local Security Policy.

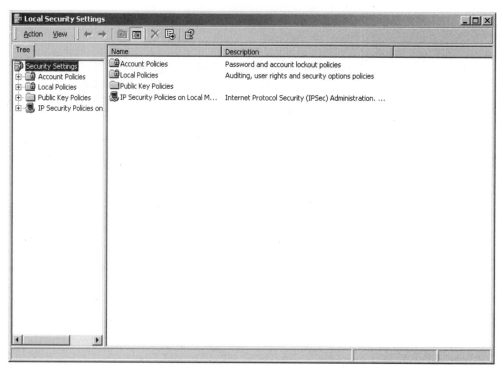

Figure 4-15   The Local Security Settings window.

3. Display the list.

In the Tree pane, expand Local Policies, and then click User Rights Assignment. In the pane on the right, you'll see a list of user rights, as shown in Figure 4-16. Use the vertical scroll bar to see the rest of the list.

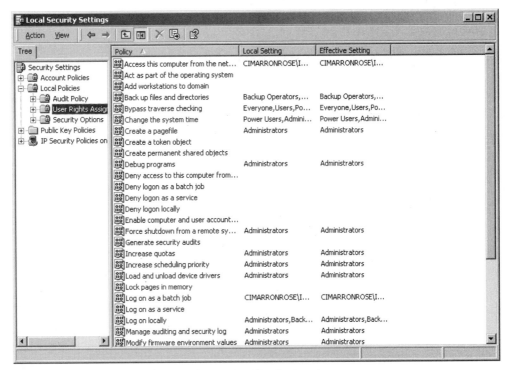

Figure 4-16 User rights in Windows 2000 Professional.

Take a minute to peruse this list. Most of these rights are self-explanatory, but it's helpful to have an idea of what's included.

Setting up user accounts

To set up a new user account on your local computer, log on as Administrator, and then follow these steps:

1. **Open the Users And Passwords dialog box, which is shown in Figure 4-17.**

   Click the Start button, click Settings, and then click Control Panel to open Control Panel. Click Users And Passwords.

Figure 4-17   The Users And Passwords dialog box.

2. Open the Add New User dialog box, which is shown in Figure 4-18.

Click the Users tab, if necessary, and then click the Add button.

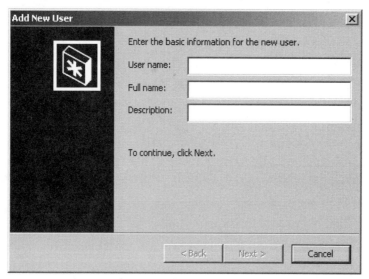

Figure 4-18   The Add New User dialog box.

3. Assign a username.

In the User Name box, enter a name for the user. The name must be unique on this computer, can be a maximum of 20 characters, and is not case-sensitive. In the Full Name box, enter the user's complete name, and then enter a description if you want. The description might be, for example, the person's position in the company. Click Next.

4. Assign the user a password.

In the Password box, type a password for the user. (Asterisks appear in place of the characters you type.) In the Confirm Password box, retype the password, and then click Next. If your network includes only Windows 2000 Professional machines, the password can be a maximum of 127 characters. If your network includes Windows 2000 Professional machines and Windows 98 or Windows 95 machines, the password should be a maximum of only 14 characters. Passwords are case-sensitive. Click Next.

5. Assign the user a level of access.

You can choose from standard access, restricted access, or another type, as you can see in Figure 4-19. Select an option, and then click Finish.

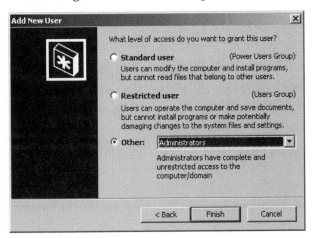

Figure 4-19   Assigning an access level to a user.

The new user is now listed in the Users For This Computer section of the Users And Passwords dialog box. To exercise more control in creating a user account, click the Advanced tab, and then follow these steps:

1. Open the Local Users And Groups window, as shown in Figure 4-20.

Click the Advanced button.

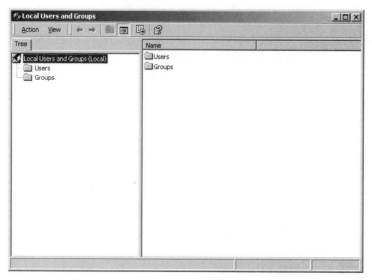

Figure 4-20   The Local Users And Groups window.

2. Open the New User dialog box, as shown in Figure 4-21.

Select Users, click the Action menu, and then click New User.

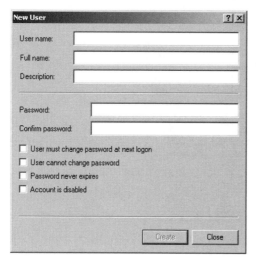

Figure 4-21   The New User dialog box.

3. **Assign a username and password.**

Enter a username, the user's full name, and enter and then confirm a password. Click check boxes to specify whether the user should change his password the next time he logs on, whether the user *can* change his password, and whether the password ever expires (it's not a good idea to check this box). As you can see in Figure 4-20, you can also use this dialog box to disable an account. When you've made your choices, click Create.

The name of the new user you just created will now appear in the right pane of the Local Users And Groups window when you select the Users folder in the Tree pane.

To enable an account you've disabled, right-click the account in the Local Users And Groups window, choose Properties from the shortcut menu to open the Properties dialog box for that account, and clear the Account Is Disabled check box.

Setting up group accounts

As you read earlier in this skill, Windows 2000 Professional creates several group accounts by default. You can, however, create other groups to satisfy organizational purposes. For example, you might want to create a group for a special project. To create a new group, follow these steps:

1. **Open the Local Users And Groups window.**

In Control Panel, click Users And Passwords to open the Users And Passwords dialog box, click the Advanced tab, and then click the Advanced button.

2. **Open the New Group dialog box, as shown in Figure 4-22.**

In the Local Users And Groups window, select Group, click the Action menu, and then click New Group.

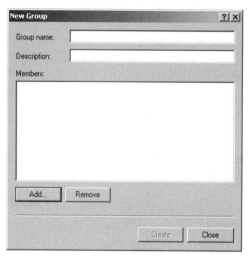

Figure 4-22   The New Group dialog box.

3. Create the group, and add members to it.

In the Group Name box, enter a name for the group, and then enter a description. To add a member, click the Add button to open the Select Users Or Groups dialog box, as shown in Figure 4-23. Select a name from the Name list, and click Add. Repeat this selection process for each person you want to add to the group, and then click OK. Back in the New Group dialog box, click Create.

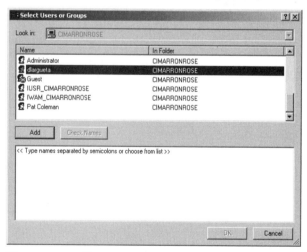

Figure 4-23   The Select Users Or Groups dialog box.

This new group now appears in the right pane of the Local Users And Groups window when you select Groups in the Tree pane.

Installing Applications

After your Windows 2000 Professional network is up and running, you'll probably want to install the applications you use most frequently. If you're wondering whether they'll work with Windows 2000 Professional, you can find out in a couple of ways.

First, you should check the constantly updated catalog of Windows 2000–compliant applications at *www.microsoft.com/windows2000/ready*. You can search by product name, product category, and company name.

You could also check with the maker of the software program to find out if there are any incompatibilities with the software and Windows 2000. This information is usually located on the company's Web site.

The final way to check whether an application will run on Windows 2000 is simply to install it and see what happens. In particular, verify that these functions work:

- Printing
- Saving files
- Exporting data
- Cutting and pasting through the Clipboard

Also run some routine tasks to find out whether their stability has been affected.

If you're considering acquiring new applications, look for those that display the Certified for Windows 2000 logo on the package.

Some applications that may not work are those developed to run on MS-DOS and Windows 3.*x*. Some Windows 95 applications won't work either. However, I've found that most MS-DOS and Windows 3.*x* programs that don't explicitly access computer hardware (games, communications software, and virus checkers are typical examples of programs that most likely won't work) will still run under Windows 2000. Moreover, while many Windows 95 programs will have trouble running under Windows 2000, a large number of Windows 98 applications do work in Windows 2000 Professional.

Network Tips and Tricks

Here are some reminders about things that are particularly important in working on a network and some tips I've discovered by working on the peer-to-peer network in my office:

- Be sure that everyone who uses your network is scrupulous about protecting their passwords. A sticky note attached to a monitor or desktop is an open invitation for someone to attempt unauthorized access.

- Network administrators frequently have a policy of forcing users to change their passwords every 30 days or so, and it's also a good idea for users to use several different passwords before reverting to one that's been used before.

- If you can't access a particular computer on your network, be sure that the computer is turned on, and then wait for a few seconds. Sometimes it takes awhile for all the computers to appear in My Network Places. If you still can't access the computer, check the simple things first: cable connections and power sources.

- If you can't access a particular drive, folder, or file, verify that the resource has been shared.

- When you're finished working for the day, shut down the system, or at the very least, log off.

- If you are connecting a Windows 2000 Professional machine to a Windows 98 machine, you need to create an account in Windows 2000 Professional that is an exact duplicate of the user logged on to the Windows 98 machine. The user name and the password must be identical.

Connecting to a Corporate Network

When you connect to a local area network at your place of business, you are probably connecting to a client/server network. If you are running Windows 2000 Professional on your desktop, you could be connecting to Windows 2000 Server or Windows NT 4 Server. When your computer starts, you'll see a message that network communications are being established. You can then log on to the system as described in Skill 1.

You can also log on to that local area network from your home network or while you're on the road, and you can do so in the following ways:

- Over a phone line

- Through a VPN tunnel

Connecting in this way is called *remote access*.

NOTE   *Remote doesn't mean from some place far from civilization; it just means away from the office.*

Using a phone line

Perhaps the most common way to access a remote network is by modem. To do this task most successfully, first make sure that your modem and the modem at the office are compatible. Of course, you also need the permission of the corporate powers that be. For security reasons, some corporations don't allow remote access to the system, but as more and more people telecommute, this is becoming less common.

To set up a dial-up connection, obtain the phone number you need to dial in to, and then follow these steps:

1. **Open the Network And Dial-Up Connections folder, as shown in Figure 4-24.**

   Click the Start button, click Settings, and then click Network And Dial-Up Connections.

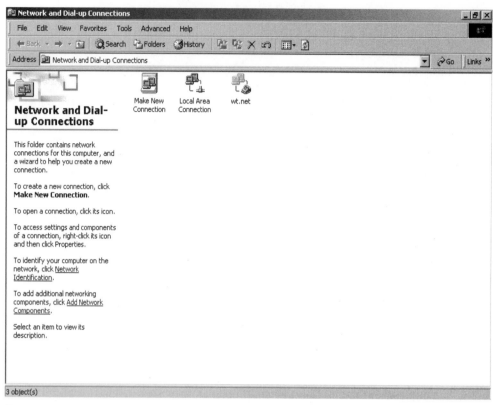

Figure 4-24 The Network And Dial-Up Connections folder.

2. Start the Network Connection Wizard, as shown in Figure 4-25.

Click the Make New Connection icon.

Figure 4-25 The Network Connection Wizard.

3. Select a network connection type.

Click Next, click the Dial-Up To Private Network option, and then click Next.

4. Tell your modem which phone number to dial.

On the Phone Number To Dial screen, as shown in Figure 4-26, enter a phone number. If you want your computer to decide how to dial in from various locations or you live in a location with multiple area codes that are all local calls, click the Use Dialing Rules check box. Click Next.

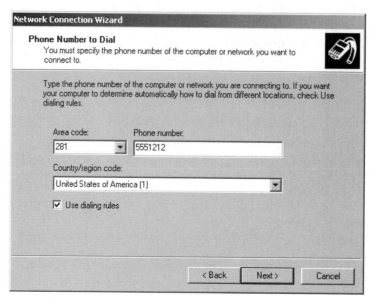

Figure 4-26 Entering a phone number.

5. Specify who can use this connection.

On the Connection Availability screen, click For All Users or Only For Myself. Click Next.

6. Name the connection.

Enter a name for this connection, which will appear in the Network And Dial-Up Connections folder, and then click Finish.

If you want to connect immediately, enter your username and password and click Dial in the Connect dialog box that now appears. If you want to connect later, click Cancel. To connect at any time, click the icon for this connection in the Network And Dial-Up Connections folder.

To delete a connection, select its icon, and press Delete.

Using a VPN tunnel

VPN stands for Virtual Private Network, a tunnel through the Internet that connects your computer to your corporate network. You can dial up almost any Internet service provider (ISP) and set up a VPN session. Because data that is transmitted via the VPN tunnel is encrypted, the data is secure.

To set up a VPN connection, you will need the host name or IP address of your corporate network, which you can obtain from your system administrator if you don't know it. Follow these steps to set up the connection:

1. **Open the Network And Dial-Up Connections folder.**

   Click the Start button, click Settings, and then click Network And Dial-Up Connections.

2. **Start the Network Connection Wizard.**

   Click the Make New Connection icon.

3. **Select a network connection type.**

   Click Next. On the Network Connection Type screen, click the Connect To A Private Network Through The Internet option. Click Next again.

4. **Specify whether to automatically dial your ISP.**

   On the Public Network screen (which appears if you have a dial-up Internet connection), shown in Figure 4-27, click the Automatically Dial This Initial Connection option if you want to establish a connection to your ISP first before connecting to your corporate network. Otherwise, click Do Not Dial The Initial Connection. Click Next.

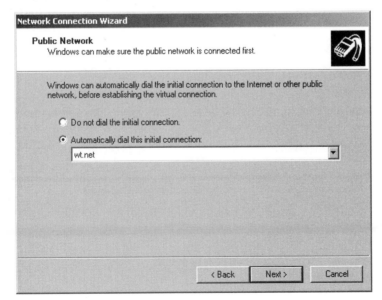

Figure 4-27   Specifying the destination address.

5. **Specify the destination address.**

In the Host Name Or IP Address box, enter the host name or address you obtained from your system administrator. A host name is something like *stephenlnelson.com,* and an IP (Internet Protocol) address is a string of numbers, such as 123.45.6.78. Click Next.

6. **Specify who can use this connection.**

On the Connection Availability screen, click For All Users or Only For Myself, and then click Next.

7. **Name the connection.**

Enter a name for this connection, which will appear in the Network And Dial-Up Connections folder, and then click Finish.

If you want to connect immediately, click Yes in the Initial Connection dialog box that now appears. If you want to connect later, click No. To connect at any time, click the icon for this connection in the Network And Dial-Up Connections folder.

To delete a connection, select its icon, and press Delete.

You can copy the connections you made for the modem or VPN by right-clicking the connection and choosing Create Copy from the shortcut menu. You can then right-click the copy and choose Properties from the shortcut menu to modify the connection for a particular situation.

Summary

Although this skill rather briskly covers a great deal of information, now you know how to set up a small network, install and use a network printer, set up user and group accounts, install applications, and connect remotely to a corporate network. Networking used to be a technical mystery that required technical mastery. Now all you need is Windows 2000 Professional and the steps outlined in this skill.

CUSTOMIZE WINDOWS 2000 PROFESSIONAL

Featuring:

- Understanding Control Panel
- Using Web View vs. Using the Classic Windows View
- Making Windows 2000 Professional More Accessible
- Setting the Date and Time
- Customizing the Display
- Adjusting the Mouse
- Adjusting the Keyboard
- Setting Regional Options
- Adding Hardware
- Adding and Removing Programs
- Personalizing the Start Menu
- Understanding User Profiles
- Looking at the Registry

You can use Windows 2000 Professional just as it comes out of the box, but as you become familiar with it, you'll probably want to tinker a bit—or maybe a lot. If you're working on a corporate network, your system administrator might have set things up so that you can't tinker with certain features. In addition, you must have permission to change some features, such as the date and time. To modify other features, you need to be logged on as Administrator. Of course, if you have a network set up in your business, you probably are the administrator, and you can do anything you want.

In Windows 2000 Professional, you use Control Panel to customize features. Any changes you make are stored in the *Registry,* which is a database that contains all the configuration information about your system. (A brief discussion of the Registry is at the end of this skill.) If you are a knowledgeable user and have some technical background, you could make the changes directly in the Registry, but that is a very risky undertaking. You can inadvertently bring down your entire network if you don't know exactly what you are doing.

Rather than use the Registry, you should use the applets in Control Panel to customize your system. This skill starts with an overview of Control Panel and then tells you step by step how to personalize certain features so that you can set up Windows 2000 Professional to work the way you want to work.

Understanding Control Panel

If you've been following along with the previous skills, you've already used Control Panel several times. The applets in Control Panel are theoretically small applications, but, as you will see, some of them are anything but small, and many are extremely powerful.

As you already know, to open Control Panel, you click the Start button, click Settings, and then click Control Panel. Figure 5-1 shows Control Panel in Large Icons view. You can also display Control Panel in Small Icons, List, and Details views. Click the View menu, and then choose a view.

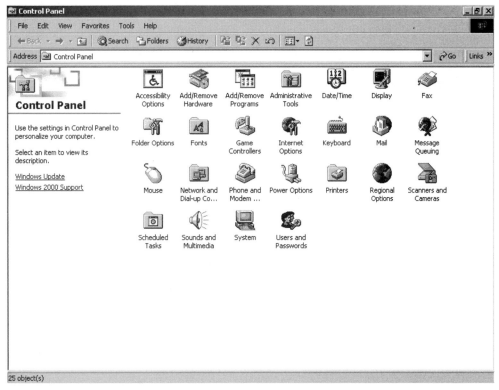

Figure 5-1   Control Panel in Large Icons view.

Notice that on the left are links to Windows Update and Windows 2000 Support. If you are connected to the Internet, clicking either of these links will take you to that Web site.

This skill does not discuss how every applet works (some are discussed in other skills), although it does cover the ones you're likely to use most often.

If you use Control Panel frequently and want quick access to the applets, you can place Control Panel on your Start menu. To do so, follow these steps:

1. Open the Taskbar And Start Menu Properties dialog box.

Click the Start button, choose Settings, choose Taskbar And Start Menu Properties from the submenu, and then click the Advanced tab.

2. Specify to expand Control Panel.

In the Start Menu Settings box, select the Expand Control Panel check box, and then click OK.

Now when you click the Start button, click Settings and then click Control Panel, you'll see a list of all the applets. Simply click an applet to open it.

Using Web View vs. Using the Classic Windows View

When you first install Windows 2000 Professional, the user interface is somewhat of a hybrid: the desktop is displayed in classic Windows view, and folders are displayed in Web view. To view the desktop as a Web page, you use the Folder Options applet in Control Panel. Follow these steps:

1. Open the Folder Options dialog box, which is shown in Figure 5-2.

In Control Panel, click Folder Options. You can also open the Folder Options dialog box in Windows Explorer by clicking the Tools menu and then clicking Folder Options.

Figure 5-2   The General tab in the Folder Options dialog box.

2. Turn on Web view.

On the General tab, click Enable Web Content On My Desktop in the Active Desktop section. In the Click Items As Follows section, click the Single-Click To Open An Item option. Click OK.

Now the icon labels on your desktop are underlined and behave like links on a Web page. If you want, you can display your home page on the desktop in Web view. To do so, right-click an empty area of the desktop, choose Active Desktop from the shortcut menu, and then click My Current Home Page on the submenu. Figure 5-3 shows my desktop in Web view and displays my home page.

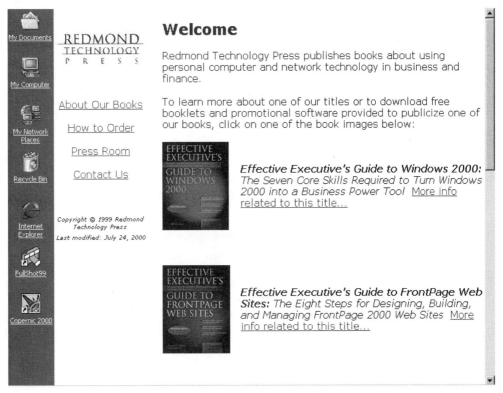

Figure 5-3 My Active Desktop.

When the Active Desktop is enabled, pointing to an object selects it, and single-clicking opens it.

Opinions vary about whether Web view or classic Windows view is better. Some Windows enthusiasts believe that Web view is the wave of the future. I don't think that it really matters which you use. Of course, if you want live Web content on the desktop, you'll need to use Web view. At any time, to return to the default, hybrid view, click the Restore Defaults button on the General tab in the Folder Options dialog box.

Making Windows 2000 Professional More Accessible

Using a computer is sometimes challenging for any of us, although it can be even more challenging if you have a disability such as a visual impairment, a mobility impairment, a hearing impairment, or cognitive or language impairments. In the United States, more than 30 million people are estimated to have a disability that makes using a computer difficult. Thus, enhancing accessibility options was key in the development of Windows 2000 Professional.

To customize the accessibility options, you can use two tools: the Accessibility Options applet in Control Panel and the Accessibility accessories.

NOTE *If you or someone in your office needs assistive technology in addition to the options provided in Windows 2000 Professional, go to the Microsoft Accessibility site (www.microsoft.com/enable/). Scroll down to the bottom of the opening page to click on a link that will take you to accessibility newsgroups. (Newsgroups are discussed in detail in the next skill.)*

Using the Accessibility Options applet

To open the Accessibility Options dialog box, click Accessibility Options in Control Panel. On the Keyboard tab, which is shown in Figure 5-4, you can customize your keyboard in the following ways:

- Click the Use StickyKeys check box if you have difficulty pressing two keys at once, such as Ctrl+Alt. To fine-tune the use of StickyKeys, click the Settings button, and use the options in the Settings For StickyKeys dialog box.

- Click the Use FilterKeys check box if you want Windows 2000 Professional to ignore short or repeated keystrokes or to slow the repeat rate. To fine-tune the use of FilterKeys, click the Settings button, and use the options in the Settings For FilterKeys dialog box.

- Click the Use ToggleKeys check box if you want to hear a sound when you press Caps Lock, Num Lock, and Scroll Lock. Click the Settings button to open the Settings For ToggleKeys dialog box, in which you can enable or disable a shortcut that activates ToggleKeys.

Figure 5-4 The Keyboard tab in the Accessibility Options dialog box.

You can use the other tabs in the Accessibility Options dialog box to adjust the sound, the display, and the mouse:

• Click the Sound tab, and then click the Use SoundSentry check box if you want a visual cue when your system generates a sound. Click the Use ShowSounds check box if you want captions for speech and sounds that an application makes.

• Click the Display tab, and then click the Use High Contrast check box if you need a display that's easier to read.

• Click the Mouse tab, and then click the Use MouseKeys check box if you want to control the mouse pointer from the numeric keypad.

• Click the General tab to specify an idle time interval after which accessibility features are turned off, to enable warning messages or sounds that signal the turning on or off of a feature, to enable an alternative mouse or keyboard device, and to select administrative options.

Using the Accessibility accessories

To activate other accessibility options, you use the Accessibility accessories. *Accessories* are applications that come with Windows 2000 Professional; Appendix A discusses some others that are of particular value to business users. To open the Accessibility accessories, click the Start button, click Programs, click Accessories, and then click Accessibility.

Using the Accessibility Wizard

Using the Accessibility Wizard is an easy way to set up accessibility options, including some that you can also set in the Accessibility Options dialog box. To start the wizard, select Accessibility Wizard from the Accessibility submenu in Accessories. You can tell the wizard what your particular disability is, and then you can follow simple onscreen instructions for ways to modify your computer for Windows 2000 Professional accordingly.

For example, start the wizard and click Next until you reach the Set Wizard Options screen, as shown in Figure 5-5. Click the I Am Blind Or Have Difficulty Seeing Things On Screen check box, and then click Next. The wizard will then step you through selecting how you want to view components such as scroll bars, icons, colors, and the mouse cursor.

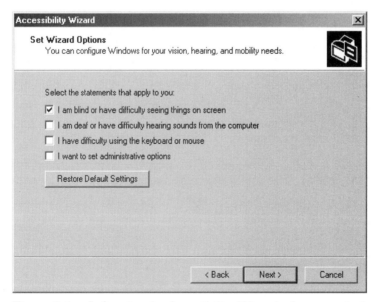

Figure 5-5 Informing the Accessibility Wizard of your particular disability.

TIP   *When you select to save your settings in the wizard, you can take the file and apply those settings to another computer.*

Using Magnifier

As you were clicking through screens in the previous section, you might have noticed a screen that let you choose to use Microsoft *Magnifier.* This utility displays a magnified portion of your screen in a separate window, as shown in Figure 5-6.

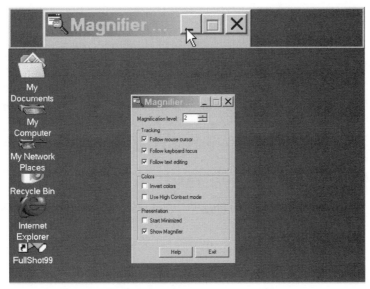

Figure 5-6   Setting up Magnifier.

To set up Magnifier, select it in the wizard, and then click Next to display the Magnifier dialog box. You can tell Magnifier to follow the mouse, the keyboard focus, or text editing. To return to Normal view, click the Exit button in the Magnifier dialog box.

Running Narrator

If you have difficulty reading the screen or if you are blind, you can enable Sam, the Windows 2000 Professional Narrator. Sam reads aloud menu commands and dialog box options, for example. Click Narrator on the Accessibility submenu to open the Narrator dialog box, which is shown in Figure 5-7. Sam reads aloud the contents of this dialog box.

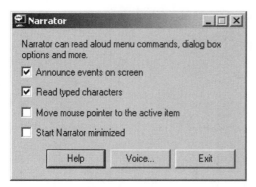

Figure 5-7   Using Narrator.

In the Narrator dialog box, click the Voice button to open the Voice Settings dialog box, in which you can modify the speed at which Sam reads and the volume and pitch of his voice. If Narrator does not perform well enough to meet your needs or cannot read some applications, you will need a more fully functional utility. You can find a list of such utilities at the Microsoft Accessibility site *(www.microsoft.com/enable/)*.

Using the onscreen keyboard

If you have a disability that makes typing difficult, you might want to check out the onscreen keyboard. You can use the mouse to type. To see how this process works, follow these steps:

1. Open Notepad.

Click the Start button, click Programs, click Accessories, click Notepad, and then maximize Notepad.

2. Open the onscreen keyboard.

Click the Start button, click Programs, click Accessories, click Accessibility, and then click On-Screen Keyboard. Your screen will look like the one shown in Figure 5-8.

Figure 5-8   Clicking the mouse to type on the screen.

3. Enter some text.

Click the keys with your mouse to enter text in Notepad. You can alternate between "typing" and choosing menu commands. When you're finished, click Close to close both Notepad and the keyboard.

TIP   *If you can't see a portion of the screen where you need to type, click the keyboard's title bar and drag the keyboard to a new location.*

Using Utility Manager

You use Utility Manager, which is shown in Figure 5-9, to start and stop Magnifier, Narrator, and On-Screen Keyboard and to specify that any of the three start automatically when Windows starts or when you start Utility Manager. To open Utility Manager, click it on the Accessibility submenu.

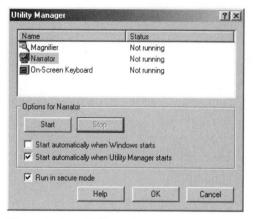

Figure 5-9   Utility Manager.

Setting the Date and Time

You set the date and time in Windows 2000 Professional in the Date/Time Properties dialog box, as shown in Figure 5-10. You can open this dialog box in a couple of ways:

- Right-click the time in the status area, and choose Adjust Date/Time from the shortcut menu.

- Click Date/Time in Control Panel.

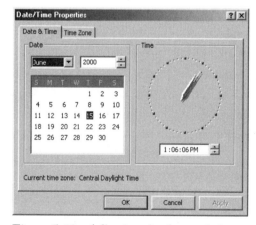

Figure 5-10   Adjusting the date and time.

To change the month, click the month drop-down list box, and select a month. To change the year, click the year spin box, and select a year. To change the time, enter a time, or click the arrows in the spin box and select a time. To change the time zone, click the Time Zone tab, and select a time zone from the drop-down list. By default, Windows 2000 Professional adjusts the time when the date arrives to go on daylight or standard time. If you don't want this to happen, clear the Automatically Adjust Clock For Daylight Saving Changes.

NOTE   *Remember that you must have permission to change the date and time if you are working on a network.*

Customizing the Display

The illustrations used to this point in the book have used the Windows Standard color scheme and have not use a graphical background on the desktop. You can be much more imaginative about the display, though, if you're so inclined. Figure 5-11 shows you just one of myriad possibilities. This screen shows the Active Desktop and the Gold Petals wallpaper that comes with Windows 2000 Professional.

Figure 5-11   A rather nonstandard desktop.

To customize the display, you use the Display Properties dialog box, which is shown in Figure 5-12. You can open this dialog box in a couple of ways:

- Right-click an empty area of the desktop and choosing Properties from the shortcut menu.

- Click Display in Control Panel.

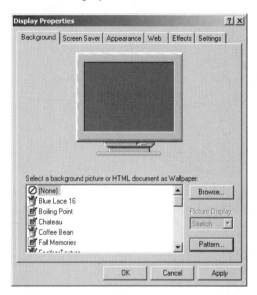

Figure 5-12   The Display Properties dialog box.

Setting the background and the wallpaper

You have many options when it comes to choosing background patterns and wallpaper. A *pattern* is a simple design that repeats; wallpaper can be anything from a picture created in a drawing program to a piece of art you download from the Internet. You can place a single picture in the center of the screen, you can tile the picture so that multiple identical images cover the screen, or you can stretch a picture so that it covers the entire screen.

Displaying a pattern

To display a pattern as a background, follow these steps:

1. **Open the Pattern dialog box, as shown in Figure 5-13.**

   In the Display Properties dialog box, set the wallpaper to None, and click the Pattern button.

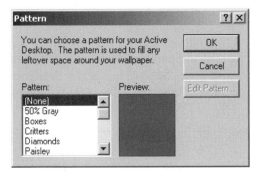

Figure 5-13   The Pattern dialog box.

2. Select a pattern.

On the Pattern list, select a pattern. You can see what it looks like in the Preview box. Click OK, and then click OK again in the Display Properties dialog box.

TIP   *For a pattern to show up, you must set wallpaper to None or set the Picture Display option to Center.*

Customizing a pattern

To customize one of the patterns that comes with Windows 2000 Professional, follow these steps:

1. Open the Pattern Editor, as shown in Figure 5-14.

In the Pattern dialog box, select a pattern, and click Edit Pattern.

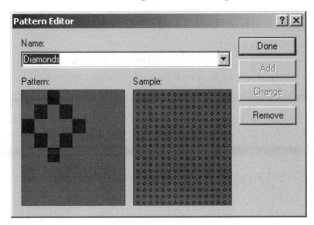

Figure 5-14   The Pattern Editor dialog box.

2. **Name and edit the pattern.**

In the Name box, enter a name for your customized pattern. The Pattern box shows an enlarged view of a single element of the pattern. Click on cells within this box to turn them on and off. The diagram in the Sample box will reflect your changes.

3. **Save the customized pattern.**

When the pattern is to your liking, click Add to save it, and then click Done. You'll see the name of your customized pattern on the Pattern list. Click OK to close the Pattern dialog box.

Choosing wallpaper

You can use any kind of digital art as wallpaper as long as it is saved as a bitmap file (it has the extension .bmp or .dib). You can also use .gif, .jpg .png images and Web pages as wallpaper, provided you allow Windows 2000 to turn on the Active Desktop feature. To use art you find on the Internet as wallpaper, right-click the art in Internet Explorer or Netscape Navigator, and choose Set As Wallpaper from the short-cut menu. To load a new bitmap file as wallpaper, follow these steps:

1. **Locate the file.**

In the Display Properties dialog box, click the Browse button to open the Browse dialog box. Switch to the folder containing the bitmap file, select it, and click OK.

2. **Apply the new wallpaper.**

Click OK in the Display Properties dialog box.

Using a screen saver

A *screen saver* is a utility that displays a specified image on the screen after the computer has been idle for a certain amount of time. Originally, screen savers were used to prevent images from being permanently imprinted on the monitor's screen. Today's monitors need no such protection, although many people continue to use screen savers because they're decorative and fun. You can also enable password protection with a screen saver to increase the security of your system—after a certain amount of time, the screen saver activates, effectively locking your system until you return and enter your login password.

To set up a screen saver, follow these steps:

1. Select a screen saver.

In the Display Properties dialog box, click the Screen Saver tab, as shown in Figure 5-15, and then click the Screen Saver drop-down list to make a selection.

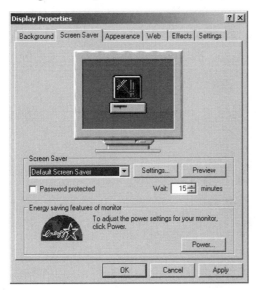

Figure 5-15   The Screen Saver tab in the Display Properties dialog box.

2. Set options for the screen saver.

You can customize some screen savers. To do so, click the Settings button to open the Settings dialog box. If the screen saver cannot be customized, you'll see a message box to that effect.

3. Specify the idle time before the screen saver kicks in.

In the Wait spin box, click the arrows to specify the number of minutes your computer will be idle before displaying the screen saver.

4. Specify password protection.

During the display of a screen saver, you can click the mouse or press any key to return to what was on the screen before the screen saver kicked in. If you don't want just anybody to be able to see what you were working on, you can turn on password protection. Click OK when you've set all the options for your screen saver.

Establishing power settings

You can also use the options available through the Screen Saver tab to enable energy-saving features for your monitor and hard drive. These options apply primarily to laptop computers, which are discussed in Appendix B. You can, though, enable energy-saving features for your desktop computer if the hardware supports them.

To set up or adjust the power settings, click the Power button on the Screen Saver tab to open the Power Options Properties dialog box, as shown in Figure 5-16.

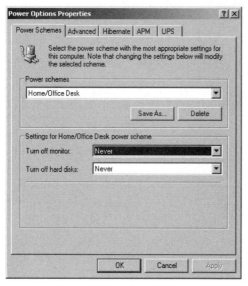

Figure 5-16   The Power Options Properties dialog box.

On the Power Schemes tab, you can do the following:

• Click the Power Schemes drop-down list to select a power scheme.

• Click the Turn Off Monitor drop-down list to specify when or whether to turn off the monitor.

• Click the Turn Off Hard Disks drop-down list to specify when or whether to turn off the hard disks.

Click the APM tab to enable Advanced Power Management if your hardware supports it, and click the UPS tab to configure an Uninterruptible Power Supply if one is installed on your system. In Appendix B, I'll discuss the other options in this dialog box.

Changing color and fonts

Earlier, this skill discussed how to change the background and wallpaper of the desktop. You can also change the color scheme and fonts for title bars, dialog boxes, menus, and other elements. To do so, you use the options on the Appearance tab of the Display Properties dialog box, which is shown in Figure 5-17.

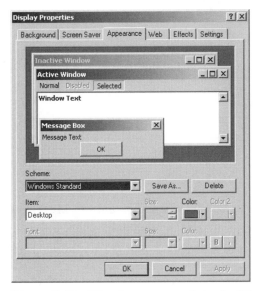

Figure 5-17   The Appearance tab in the Display Properties dialog box.

- To change the scheme, click the Scheme drop-down list, and select a new scheme. The box displays Windows elements in the scheme you've selected so that you can preview it before you commit to use it.

- To change the color of a particular Windows element, click the Item drop-down list, and select the item. Depending on the item, you can change its color (or colors) and the font and size of the text and specify whether you want the text bold or italic.

Changing the Web settings

Earlier, this skill showed you how to enable the Active Desktop using the Folder Options dialog box. You can also enable the Active Desktop on the Web tab of the Display Properties dialog box, which is shown in Figure 5-18.

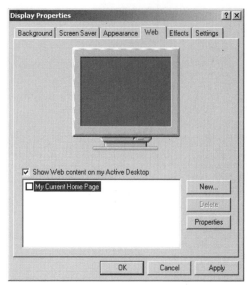

Figure 5-18   The Web tab in the Display Properties dialog box.

To enable the Active Desktop, click the Show Web Content On My Active Desktop check box. To display your current home page on your desktop, click the My Current Home Page check box. To display the settings for your current home page, click the Properties button to open the Properties dialog box for your home page.

Changing icons and other visual effects

You can change the icon associated with some desktop icons, including My Computer, My Documents, My Network Place, and the full or empty Recycle Bin, and you can change visual effects, such as the size of icons and the number of colors in which icons are displayed. To do any of these things, you use the options on the Effects tab in the Display Properties dialog box, which is shown in Figure 5-19.

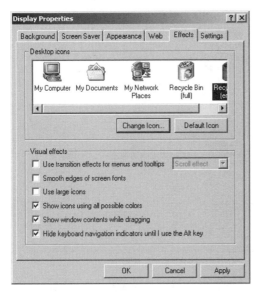

Figure 5-19 The Effects tab in the Display Properties dialog box.

To change one of the desktop icons, click the Change Icon button to open the Change Icon dialog box, select a new icon, and click OK. To change a visual effect, click its check box.

Changing the number of colors and the screen resolution

This skill has looked at numerous ways you can customize the display in Windows 2000 Professional, but it is far from finished. You can also change the number of colors that are displayed and the screen resolution; to do so, you use the Settings tab in the Display Properties dialog box, as shown in Figure 5-20.

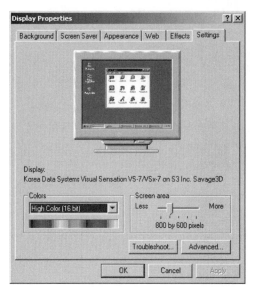

Figure 5-20 The Settings tab in the Display Properties dialog box.

The maximum number of colors depends on your monitor and your display adapter. To see the available options, click the Colors drop-down list. If you choose 256 colors, that's how many colors are displayed. The High Color setting displays more than 65,000 colors, and the True Color setting displays more than 16 million colors.

Resolution is the number of pixels (dots) on the screen and the number of colors that can be displayed at the same time. The higher the resolution, the smaller elements appear on the screen. If you have a small monitor, therefore, you'll want to stick with a lower resolution. Here are some common settings and the monitors on which they are best displayed:

- 640 by 480 is a standard Video Graphics Adapter (VGA) display that is quite readable for most people on a 14- or 15-inch monitor.

- 800 by 600 is a super VGA display. On a 15-inch monitor, this setting is really small, although it's quite readable on a 17-inch monitor.

- 1024 by 768, the upper limit of Super VGA, is readable on a 17-inch monitor if you have good eyesight.

- 1280 by 1024 is a resolution for large monitors. You can really read the text at this resolution only on a 17-inch or larger monitor.

To change the resolution, you simply move the pointer on the Screen Area slider bar.

To change the size in which fonts are displayed on your screen, click the Advanced button, and use the options in the Properties dialog box for your monitor. On the General tab, click the Font Size drop-down list to specify small or large fonts. Select Other if you want a custom font size. The Custom Font Size dialog box opens, and you can use it to scale fonts and set a custom font size.

By default, Windows 2000 Professional does not restart when you change the display settings. This setting usually works well, although if you find that some programs aren't operating properly, reboot your computer. If you always want the computer to reboot when you change the display settings, check that option on the General tab in the Properties dialog box for your monitor.

Adjusting the Mouse

You can make some adjustments to the mouse by using the Accessibility Wizard, which is described earlier in this skill. Most often, though, you'll use the Mouse applet in Control Panel.

If you are left-handed, your first step after installing Windows 2000 Professional might have been to switch the mouse buttons, and you quickly found that you do this by clicking Mouse in Control Panel to open the Mouse Properties dialog box, as shown in Figure 5-21.

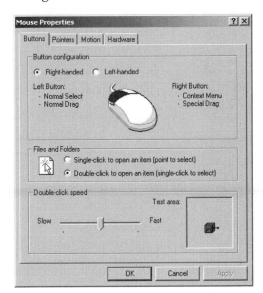

Figure 5-21 The Mouse Properties dialog box.

To switch mouse buttons, simply click the Left-Handed or Right-Handed option button. If you would rather single-click than double-click to open files and folders, click that option in the Files And Folders section. To adjust the double-click speed, adjust the Double-Click Speed slider bar. You'll see the speed change in the test area so that you can preview before you implement the change.

You use the other tabs in the Mouse Properties dialog box to do the following:

- Select a pointer scheme or customize a pointer in the Pointer tab.

- Adjust the speed and acceleration of your pointer in the Motion tab. You can also specify that the pointer moves directly to the default button in dialog boxes.

- If your mouse isn't behaving properly, click the Hardware tab, and then click Troubleshoot to start the Mouse Troubleshooter in Help.

Adjusting the Keyboard

When you install Windows 2000 Professional, the operating system recognizes your keyboard, and you don't normally need to tinker with the keyboard settings. You can, however, use the options in the Keyboard Properties dialog box, which is shown in Figure 5-22, to adjust the character repeat rate, the cursor blink rate, and the keyboard layout for other languages and to troubleshoot your keyboard.

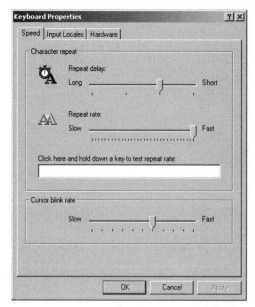

Figure 5-22 The Keyboard Properties dialog box.

On the Speed tab, click the pointer on the slider bars to set the repeat delay, the repeat rate, and the cursor blink rate. If you use multiple languages, use the options on the Input Locales tab to set them up. You can also specify whether the Caps Lock key is turned off when you press Caps Lock again or when you press the Shift key. The Hardware tab contains information about your keyboard. If you are having problems with your keyboard, press the Troubleshoot button to start the Keyboard Troubleshooter in Help. Click Properties to display the Properties dialog box for your keyboard.

Setting Regional Options

During the installation of Windows 2000 Professional, you chose a location, and then settings were established for that locale, including the display of numbers, currencies, times, and dates. To change the locale, and thus these settings, you use the Regional Options applet, which is shown in Figure 5-23.

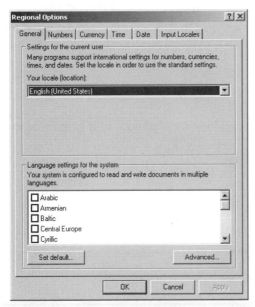

Figure 5-23 The Regional Options dialog box.

To change the settings, select a location from the Your Locale drop-down list. When you then click the other tabs, you'll see the default settings for that location, which you can customize if necessary. On the General tab, you can also specify a language setting for your system. If a check box contains a check, that language group is installed on your system. To install a language group, click its check box. Only Administrators can install a language group.

Adding Hardware

The time will surely come when you need to upgrade your system, perhaps by adding another hard drive, a faster modem, or a scanner. If you work on a corporate network, your system administrator and some technicians will in all likelihood handle this task. If you are your own system administrator in a small organization, the task will be up to you.

Adding a piece of hardware to your system involves four main steps:

1. Acquire the hardware.

2. Connect the hardware to your computer and turn it on.

3. Load the appropriate device driver.

4. Configure the hardware.

A piece of advice about step 1: If at all possible, obtain a device that is Plug and Play compliant. Windows 2000 Professional recognizes and configures Plug-and-Play devices automatically. As you will see later in this section, that saves you lots of time and aggravation. Basically, you don't have to bother with steps 3 and 4 in the preceding list.

To install new Plug-and-Play hardware, turn off your computer, and follow these steps:

TIP   *If you're adding a USB or Firewire device, all you need to do is plug the device in and turn it on—you don't need to turn your computer off first.*

1. **Connect the device.**

   Follow the manufacturer's instructions.

2. **Let Windows 2000 Professional do the rest.**

   Turn your computer back on to restart Windows 2000 Professional, which will locate the new hardware and configure it.

If for whatever reason you're installing a device that is not Plug and Play, you'll need to use the Add/Remove Hardware applet in Control Panel. First, turn off your computer, connect the device, and then turn your computer back on to restart Windows 2000 Professional. In Control Panel, click Add/Remove Hardware to start the Add/Remove Hardware Wizard, as shown in Figure 5-24.

NOTE   *You must log on as an administrator to run the Add/Remove Hardware Wizard.*

Figure 5-24 The Add/Remove Hardware Wizard.

At the Welcome screen, click Next, and then follow these steps:

1. Tell the Wizard that you are adding a device.

On the Choose A Hardware Task screen, click the Add/Troubleshoot A Device option, and then click Next.

2. Select the device.

On the Choose A Hardware Device screen, select the device from the list, and click Next.

3. Find the device.

On the Find New Hardware screen, you can choose to let Windows 2000 Professional search for the device, or you can select it from a list. If you let Windows search for the device, a status monitor indicates the progress of the search. If you want to select the device from the list, choose that option, and then click Next. Select the device from the list, and then click Next.

What happens next depends on the type of device you are installing, although the Wizard walks you through the steps. Follow the onscreen instructions.

Adding and Removing Programs

To add and remove Windows applications and Windows components, you use the Add/Remove Programs applet in Control Panel. To add an application that everyone on your system can use, you need to log on as an administrator. To add an application for a particular user on the system, log on with that person's username.

Adding a new program

To add a new program, follow these steps:

1. Open the Add/Remove Programs dialog box.

In Control Panel, click Add/Remove Programs, and then click the Add New Programs icon. You'll see the screen shown in Figure 5-25.

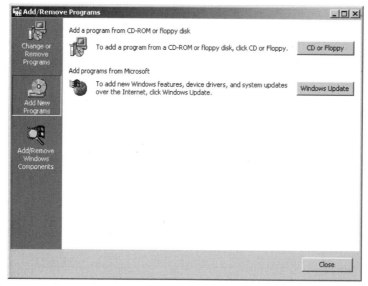

Figure 5-25   The Add/Remove Programs dialog box.

2. Install from a CD or a floppy.

Click the CD Or Floppy button. A wizard then guides you through installing and configuring the new application. Follow the onscreen instructions.

NOTE   *If you are connected to the Internet, you can click the Windows Update button to go to a Microsoft Web site where you can download files for new Windows 2000 Professional features, system updates, and device drivers.*

Changing and removing programs

From time to time, you will want to get rid of existing programs that you've installed or change them. If you've been a longtime user of Windows, you might remember the day when you could simply locate the executable file for a program and delete it. The only safe way to remove a program in Windows 2000 Professional is to use the Add/Remove Programs applet, which calls the Windows Installer into service.

To change or remove a Windows program, click the Change Or Remove Programs button in the Add/Remove Programs dialog box, and follow the onscreen instructions.

Adding and removing Windows components

To add or remove a Windows 2000 Professional component, you will need to be logged on as an administrator, and you will need your installation CD at hand (or access to a network share with the installation files). Insert it in the drive, and then click Add/Remove Windows Components in the Add/Remove Programs dialog box to start the Windows Components Wizard, as shown in Figure 5-26. To add or remove a component, follow the onscreen instructions.

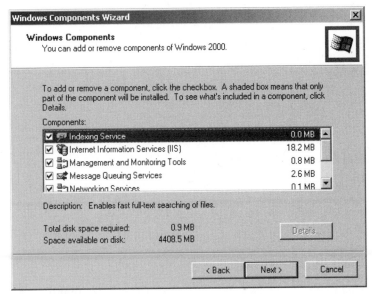

Figure 5-26   The Windows Components Wizard.

Personalizing the Start Menu

The first part of this skill showed you how to turn the Control Panel into a cascading menu, although you can personalize your Start menu in many other ways. For example, if you are working on a big document that is stored on your network, you can easily place it on the Start menu. Follow these steps:

1. **Open the Taskbar And Start Menu Properties dialog box.**

   Right-click an empty area of the taskbar, and choose Properties.

2. **Open the Create Shortcut dialog box, which is shown in Figure 5-27.**

   In the Taskbar And Start Menu Properties dialog box, click the Advanced tab, and then click Add.

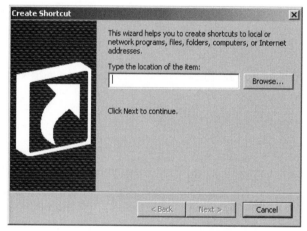

Figure 5-27   The Create Shortcut dialog box.

3. **Enter the location of the document.**

   Enter the pathname of the file, or click Browse to locate it, and then click Next.

4. **Select the folder for the document.**

   Click the Start Menu folder, and then click Next.

5. **Name the shortcut.**

   Enter the document name that will appear on the Start menu, and then click Finish.

To remove an item you've added from the Start menu, right-click the item, and then choose Delete from the shortcut menu.

You can also personalize the Start menu in some other ways, using the Advanced tab, which is shown in Figure 5-28.

Figure 5-28 The Advanced tab in the Taskbar And Start Menu Properties dialog box.

Use the vertical scroll bar to peruse the items on the Start Menu Settings list. Here are some examples of ways to place items on the Start menu and skip some steps involved in certain tasks:

- Click the Display Logoff check box to place that item on the Start menu and bypass the Shut Down Windows dialog box when you want to log off the system.

- Click the Display Favorites check box to place that item on the Start menu and open a favorite Web site without first opening Internet Explorer. (The next skill describes Internet Explorer.)

- Click Expand Printers to display the items in your Printers folder when you click Settings and then click Printers.

You get the idea.

Understanding User Profiles

A *user profile* is a collection of settings that are applied each time you log on to the system. These settings include the following:

- Your Start menu options.

- The desktop icons you've selected.

- The display colors you've specified.

- The wallpaper, background, and screen saver you chose.

- Any accessibility options you've set up.

- Sounds you've chosen to associate with system events.

- A special mouse cursor you want to use.

In other words, a user profile contains the settings for all the customization you've put in place using any of the tools already discussed in this skill.

You can set up three types of user profiles:

- A *local* user profile was created the first time you logged on to your local hard drive after installing Windows 2000 Professional. When you then logged off, any changes you made to the display, accessibility options, and so on were stored in your user profile. If more than one user has logged on to your system, you will find multiple user profiles displayed on the list on the User Profiles tab in the System Properties dialog box. (More about this in a moment.) User profiles are commonly used on standalone or peer-to-peer systems.

- A *roaming* user profile is created for you by the system administrator, and the profile follows you to any computer you log on to on the network. Roaming user profiles are common on client/server networks.

- A *mandatory* user profile can also be created by the system administrator. This profile specifies required settings for individuals and groups. If mandatory user profiles are in use, you cannot log on to the system until the appropriate mandatory user profile is found and loaded.

If you are the system administrator and new users use your machine, you can create a user profile for a new user. Follow these steps:

1. **Set up a custom profile on the user's computer.**

   Log on as the new user, modify the display, wallpaper, and so on, and then log off.

2. **Open the System Properties dialog box.**

   Log back on to your computer as Administrator, and right-click My Computer to open the System Properties dialog box. Click the User Profiles tab, which is shown in Figure 5-29.

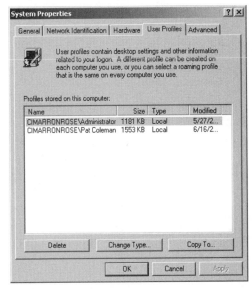

Figure 5-29   The User Profiles tab in the System Properties dialog box.

3. **Copy the Administrator user profile to the default user profile.**

   Highlight the profile you want to copy, and click the Copy To button to open the Copy To dialog box, which is shown in Figure 5-30.

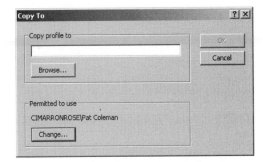

Figure 5-30   The Copy To dialog box.

4. Enter the path.

In the Copy Profile To box, enter *%SYSTEMROOT%\Documents & Settings\Default User*, and then click OK.

Looking at the Registry

The beginning of this skill mentioned that all the customization changes you make using the Control Panel applets are stored in the Registry, and you were warned about tinkering directly with it. To be an informed user of Windows 2000 Professional, however, you should at least know what it looks like and what it contains. Besides, simply opening the Registry, taking a peek, and closing it back up is definitely not a risky business.

Follow these steps to open the Registry:

1. Open the Run dialog box.

Click the Start button, and then click Run.

2. Open the Registry.

In the Open box, type *regedit*. You'll see a screen similar to what's shown in Figure 5-31.

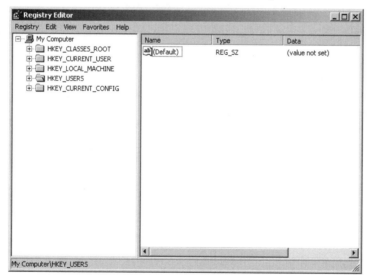

Figure 5-31   The Windows Registry Editor.

In the pane on the left are six folders, each of which contains specific information about your computer system. To see the contents of a folder, click the plus sign to expand it. To be on the safe side, click the Close button.

Summary

Now you have a great deal of information at your fingertips if you want to get busy customizing Windows 2000 Professional. This skill has covered some of the Control Panel applets, including Accessibility Options, Add/Remove Hardware, Add/Remove Programs, Date/Time, Display, Keyboard, Mouse, and Regional Options. It also looked at a few other ways to customize the system—by modifying the Start menu, using user profiles, and displaying the desktop in Web view or classic Windows view.

Skill 6

USE THE INTERNET

Featuring:

- Getting Connected
- Browsing the Web with Internet Explorer
- Managing E-Mail with Outlook Express
- Managing Your Electronic Office

Although it is impossible for anyone to know how many people are connected to the Internet, according to *The World Almanac and Book of Facts 2000*, in mid-1999 some 200 million people around the world were using the Internet. It is estimated that by 2005 that number will increase to 1 billion. A report published in mid-2000 by MMXI Europe, a Web measurement company, said that Internet users in major markets log on to the Web more than 11 days each month and stay connected, on average, for more than 53 minutes each time.

When Esther Dyson, an Internet sage and venture capitalist, was asked recently about the future of the Internet, she said simply that in order to stay competitive, every business would need a presence on the Internet.

This skill looks at the two tools primarily responsible for the popularity of the Internet: the Web browser and electronic mail (e-mail). Both Microsoft Internet Explorer (the Web browser) and Microsoft Outlook Express (a mail and news reader) are integral to Windows 2000 Professional. Before you can use either of them to connect with the world, though, you need an account on the Internet, so this skill looks briefly at that topic and then turns to the details of using Internet Explorer and Outlook Express.

Getting Connected

You might recall that Skill 4 listed the steps for connecting a home office network to a corporate network in two ways. One of those ways, a VPN tunnel, involved using the Internet. In the past, setting up a connection to the Internet was a fairly complicated procedure, although that is no longer the case. In Windows 2000 Professional, the Internet Connection Wizard walks you through the steps, as it did when you set up those connections in Skill 4.

Before you can set up your connection to the Internet, you need an account with an Internet service provider (ISP). The Internet Connection Wizard can help you find one, or you can find services advertised in your local newspaper, or you can use one of the many commercial services whose setup CDs are bound into periodicals. Most offer unlimited modem access for around $20/month. If you're connecting via cable modem or DSL the fee will be more expensive. To set up your account, you will need the following information from your ISP:

- Your username and password
- The phone number to dial in to your ISP
- The name of your incoming mail server
- The name of your outgoing mail server

If you haven't yet set up a connection, you'll have a Connect To The Internet icon on your desktop, and you can simply click the icon to start the Internet Connection Wizard. If you've already set up a connection, you can start the Internet Connection Wizard in the following ways:

- Click the Start button, click Programs, click Accessories, click Communications, and then click Internet Connection Wizard.

- Click the Start button, click Settings, click Control Panel, and then click Internet Options to open the Internet Properties dialog box. Click the Connections tab, and then click the Setup button.

- In Internet Explorer, click the Tools menu, click Internet Options to open the Internet Options dialog box, click the Connection tab, and then click the Setup button.

Regardless of which method you use, you'll see the Welcome screen, as shown in Figure 6-1.

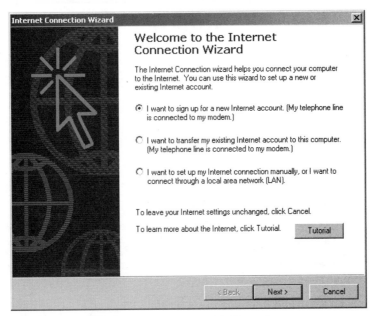

Figure 6-1 The Internet Connection Wizard.

To create a new dial-up connection, obtain an account and then follow these steps:

1. Specify the type of account you want to create.

On the Welcome screen, select I Want To Set Up My Internet Connection Manually, Or I Want To Connect Through A Local Area Network (LAN), and click Next.

2. Specify the type of connection.

On the Setting Up Your Internet Connection screen, click the I Connect Through A Phone Line And A Modem option, and then click Next.

3. Provide information about your Internet account.

Enter the phone number of your ISP, click Next, enter the username and password provided by your ISP, click Next, enter an identifying name for your connection, and click Next.

4. Set up an e-mail account.

Follow the onscreen instructions.

5. Complete the wizard.

When you have provided all your e-mail account information, click Finish, and then click Close to close the wizard and connect to the Internet.

Browsing the Web with Internet Explorer

You can open Internet Explorer in the following ways:

- Click the Launch Internet Explorer Browser button on the Quick Launch toolbar.

- Double-click the Internet Explorer shortcut on the desktop.

- Click the Start button, click Programs, and then click Internet Explorer.

The first time you open Internet Explorer, you'll see a page similar to the one shown in Figure 6-2, which shows the MSN page. You can retain this start page or select any other. The steps are listed later in this skill.

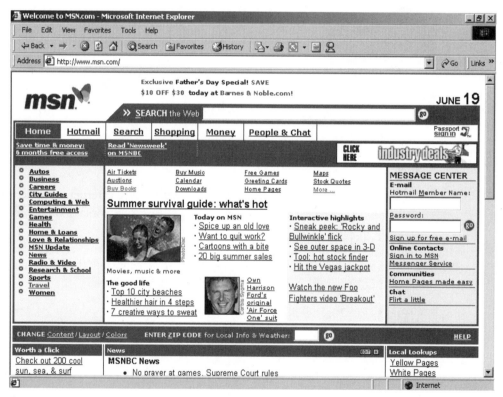

Figure 6-2 The default start page.

You can also open Internet Explorer from any document that includes a hyperlink. For example, if you receive an e-mail message that contains a URL in the body, simply click the URL to open that page in Internet Explorer. In addition, in Windows Explorer, clicking a filename that ends in .htm or .html opens that file in Internet Explorer.

NOTE *HTML (HyperText Markup Language) is the programming language used to create Web pages. To take a look at the underlying HTML for a Web page, open the page in Internet Explorer, click the View menu, and then click Source.*

A word about URLs

URL, or *Uniform Resource Locator,* is an address for a resource on the Internet. It actually represents a string of numbers called an Internet Protocol (IP) address. Because it's much easier for humans to remember names rather than numbers, we typically use URLs.

A URL is composed of a protocol, the name of the server (the host name) on which the resource resides, the domain name of the company and, optionally, the path to the resource and its filename. For example, in the URL *http://www.redtechpress.com*, http is the protocol (in this case, Hypertext Transfer Protocol), www is the host name of the server, redtechpress.com is the domain name. Such a URL might also include the path, such as /catalog, and the name of a document, such as /index.html. You frequently see URLs in various media as simply *www.redtechpress.com*. Internet Explorer and other Web browsers assume the use of the http protocol unless you specify otherwise. Another less frequently seen protocol is File Transfer Protocol (FTP); an FTP server contains programs and files that users can download.

The final part of the server name in our example, .com refers to the domain type. Seven domain types are now recognized:

- .com is a commercial organization.

- .edu is an educational institution; for example, a university.

- .gov is an entity that is part of the U.S. government.

- .int is an international organization, such as the United Nations.

- .mil is a branch of the U.S. military.

- .net is a network organization.

- .org is a nonprofit organization.

You pronounce the domain part of a URL as "dot com," "dot edu," "dot gov," and so on. You have no doubt seen references to dot-coms, which are businesses that in recent years have sprung up on the Internet. These are not simply businesses that have a Web site, but rather businesses that exist entirely on the Internet. One of the first and perhaps the most successful, if not the most profitable, was Amazon.com. Initially the mission of Amazon.com was to sell books, at a discount, over the Internet, and it billed itself as the world's largest bookstore. Now Amazon sells everything from books to software to gardening tools.

Mid-2000 found many dot-coms in trouble. Forrester Research, a leader in compiling Internet and business statistics, predicted that by 2001 most dot-coms would go out of business. The reason, according to some dot-com CEOs, is that the focus was on acquiring an audience at all costs—regardless of the costs.

Although the Internet is a seductive medium, it's probably safe to assume that there's no substitute for a well-designed and carefully thought-out business plan.

Understanding the Internet Explorer window

The components of the Internet Explorer window are much like those in other Windows applications. You'll see vertical and horizontal scroll bars as necessary, and you can size portions of the window by clicking and dragging and display a ScreenTip by pointing to a button. This list describes some other components:

- The title bar, at the top of the window, displays the name of the current Web page or other file that is open.

- The menu bar, just beneath the title bar, contains a set of menus, many of which appear in other Windows applications.

- The Standard toolbar, just beneath the menu bar, contains several buttons that correspond to items on the menu bar as well as the Back, Forward, and Home navigation buttons.

- The Address bar, beneath the Standard toolbar, is used to enter a URL or filename. You can also click the drop-down arrow to select a URL.

- The Links bar, a drop-down list on the far right side of the Address bar, contains a short list of preselected hyperlinks. You can add to this list.

- The activity indicator, at the far right of the menu bar, is animated when Internet Explorer is sending or receiving data.

- The main window displays the resource you most recently accessed.

- The status bar is at the bottom of the screen. When you choose a menu command, the status bar displays a description of what it does. When you point to a link, the status bar displays its URL. When you click a link, the status bar displays a series of messages related to the progress of finding and opening that resource.

- The security zone is at the far right of the status bar and displays the active security zone. Security zones are discussed in detail later in this skill.

Navigating the Web

After you open Internet Explorer, you can start exploring the Web immediately. All you have to do is click a link or enter on the Address bar a URL you've gleaned from TV or someone's business card. You can, however, use several techniques to make the time you spend connected to the Internet more efficient.

Using the Address bar

Sometimes when you start to enter a URL, it completes itself for you. This is the AutoComplete feature at work. If AutoComplete enters the URL you want, simply press Enter to go to that resource. If not, continue typing.

AutoComplete also works in other fields you fill in on a Web page, such as search queries, a list of stock quotes, and information you supply when you purchase items over the Internet, for example. This feature can be handy, and you do not need to worry about security when you use AutoComplete. The information you originally enter is encrypted (encoded) and stored on your computer. It is not accessible to Web sites. (Sometimes you'll even see the encryption displayed on your screen before the information is sent out.)

If you've entered a URL (perhaps a lengthy one) and then want to use only part of it to try to access a resource, place the cursor on the Address bar, hold down the Control key, and press the right or left arrow to jump forward or backward to the next separator character (the slashes and dots, for example).

TIP   *Another time-saving trick you can use when entering a .com address is to simply type the name of the company (such as* microsoft*) and then press Control-Enter—this automatically fills in the* www *and the* .com *for you (yielding* www.microsoft.com, *in this example).*

You can use the Address bar to do more than find a resource on the Internet. You can also run a program from the Address bar (for example, type *C:\Program Files\NetMeeting\conf*), and you can find a file. For example, if you enter a drive letter and press Enter, you'll see a screen similar to the one shown in Figure 6-3. You can click a folder to open subfolders and files.

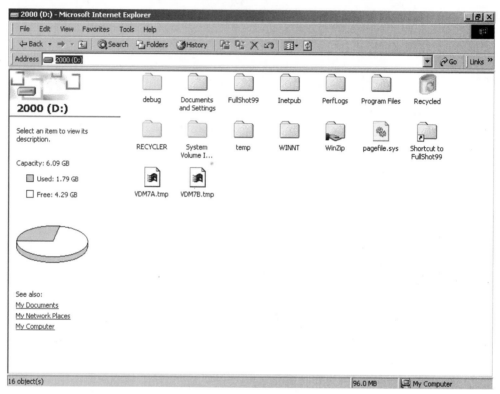

Figure 6-3   Looking for a file from the Address bar.

Following and adding links

A link can be a word, a phrase, an image, or a symbol that forms a connection with a resource that can be located on your local computer, your local network, or the Internet. In Internet Explorer, textual links are usually underlined and in a different color from normal text. You know that something is a link if the pointer becomes a hand with a pointing finger when you place the mouse cursor over it.

To follow a link, of course, you simply click it. If you find something that you know you'll want to revisit, you can place a link to it on the Links bar or add it to your Favorites list, which is discussed next. To add a link to the Links bar, simply drag the link there. To remove a link from the Links bar, right-click it and choose Delete from the shortcut menu. To rearrange items on the Links bar, drag an item to a new location.

By default, the Links bar contains the following links:

- Clicking Customize Links opens a page on the Microsoft Web site that contains information about how to add, remove, and rearrange items on the Links bar.

- Clicking Free HotMail opens a Web page where you can sign up for an e-mail account.

- Clicking Windows takes you to the Microsoft Windows site.

TIP   *If you ever lose track of where you are when following links, you can click Home to return to your start page, click Back to return to the page you last visited, or click Forward to return to the page you visited before you clicked the Back button.*

Working with your favorites

As mentioned, you can also keep track of sites you want to revisit by adding them to your Favorites list. (In some other browsers, favorites are called bookmarks.)

Keeping track of favorite sites

You can add sites to your Favorites list in two ways: Use the Favorites menu, or click the Favorites button on the toolbar.

To use the Favorites menu, follow these steps:

1. Open the Add Favorite dialog box, as shown in Figure 6-4.

Click the Favorites menu, and then click Add To Favorites.

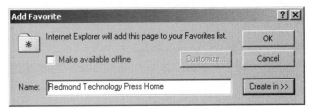

Figure 6-4   The Add Favorite dialog box.

2. Add the site to the list.

In the Name box, accept the suggested name, or type another name, and click OK.

To store a favorite site in a particular folder, click Create In to open the Create In list, and select a folder. To create a new folder, click New Folder to open the Create New Folder dialog box, type a name for the folder, and click OK.

If you know that the contents of a site will not change frequently, you can click the Make Available Offline check box. In this way, you can access the site when you aren't connected to the Internet. For example, suppose you find a lengthy report that contains facts and figures you want to be able to access easily and quickly, and you know that the report is published as of a certain date and will not change. Make it available offline.

You can also add a favorite site by clicking the Favorites button to open the Favorites bar, as shown in Figure 6-5. Click the Add button to open the Add Favorite dialog box, and then follow step 2.

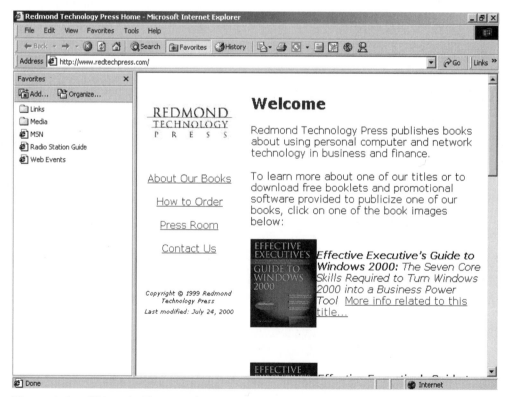

Figure 6-5   Using the Favorites bar.

Here are some other ways you can add sites to your Favorites list:

- Right-click a link, and click Add To Favorites from the shortcut menu.

- Right-click the current page outside a link, and choose Add To Favorites from the shortcut menu.

- Drag and drop a link on a Web page to the Favorites button.

Managing the Favorites list

If you just keep adding sites to the Favorites list without any sense of organization, you'll soon have links to lots of sites but you might not be able to put your cursor on one quickly. Here are some tips for managing the Favorites list:

- Create folders for collections of similar sites or for sites you want to access for a particular project.

- Weed out sites you no longer need to access. Right-click the item, and choose Delete from the shortcut menu.

- To move an item to another place in the list or to another folder, click and drag it to a new location.

- To create a new folder from the Favorites list, click Organize to open the Organize Favorites dialog box, and then click Create Folder.

- To rename a favorite, right-click it, choose Rename from the shortcut menu, type the new name, and press Enter.

Backtracking

Another way to find out where you've been and return there is to use the History list. Follow these steps:

1. **Open the History folder, which is shown in Figure 6-6.**

   Click the History button on the toolbar.

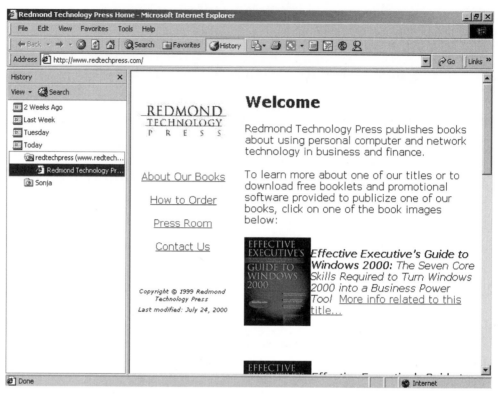

Figure 6-6   Using the History list.

2. Select a view.

Click the View menu, and then choose By Date, By Site, By Most Visited, or By Order Most Visited Today. You can also open a list of sites you visited yesterday, last week, two weeks ago, and three weeks ago.

3. Search for a site.

Click the Search button to open the Search For box, enter a term or a phrase, and click Search Now.

TIP   *For quick access to a site, place a shortcut to it on the desktop. With the page open in Internet Explorer, right-click an empty area, and choose Create Shortcut from the shortcut menu.*

Sending pages and links

When you run across a page you want to share with a colleague, you can send the page or a link to it. Simply click the Mail button on the toolbar, and click Send A Link or

Send Page. The New Message window will open with the link or the pages inserted in the body of the message. (The latter part of this skill discusses how to send messages in Outlook Express.)

Listening to a Webcast

One component of the Internet Explorer window that I didn't mention earlier is the Radio bar. It is not displayed by default, although you can display it and then use it to directly access radio stations throughout the United States and around the world.

TIP   *The quality of your listening experience will depend on your speakers, your system, and the speed at which you access the Internet. A speed of at least 56Kbps is recommended.*

To listen to a Webcast, follow these steps:

1. Display the Radio toolbar, which is shown in Figure 6-7.

Click the View menu, click Toolbars, and then click Radio.

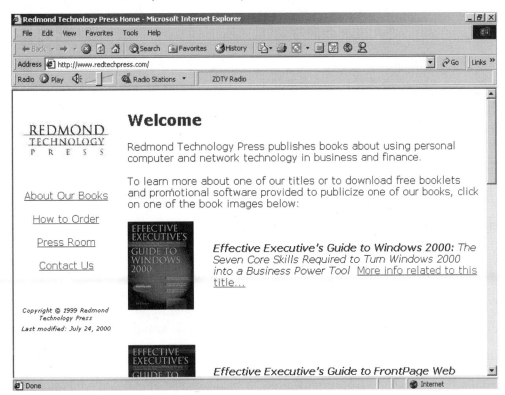

Figure 6-7   Using the Radio toolbar.

2. Locate a station.

Click Radio Stations, and then click Radio Station Guide to open the WindowsMedia.com site. Click a button to select a station.

The station's home page loads while the station is being found. To adjust the volume, move the slider on the Volume Control. To turn the radio off, click the Stop button on the Radio toolbar.

Saving and printing

You can save a Web page as a file on your local drive or on your network. To save a Web page that is open in Internet Explorer, follow these steps:

1. Open the Save Web Page dialog box, which is shown in Figure 6-8.

Click the File menu, and then click Save As.

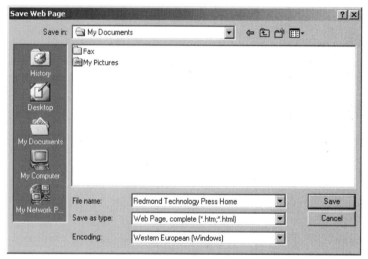

Figure 6-8   Saving a Web page.

2. Select a folder, a file name, and a type.

In the Save In box, select a folder in which to save the page. In the File Name box, accept the name that's suggested or enter another name. In the Save As Type box, select a file type. If you want to save a file with a character set other than Western European, click the drop-down Encoding list, and select a character set.

TIP   *Most Web pages include a number of images and other files. When you save a Web page using the default file format—Web Page, Complete, Internet Explorer creates a directory to store all of these files. If you would rather have the Web page be self-contained choose the Web Archive, Single File, or the Web Page, HTML only options.*

3. Save the file.

Click the Save button.

To save a Web page without opening it, right-click its link, choose Save Target As to download the file, and open the Save As dialog box. Follow steps 2 and 3 in the preceding set of steps.

To save a portion of a page and place it in another document, follow these steps:

1. Make your selection, and copy it.

Select what you want, and press Ctrl+C.

2. Insert your selection in another document.

Open the other document, place the insertion point where you want the text, and press Ctrl+V.

To save an image from a Web page, follow these steps:

1. Select the image.

Right-click the image, and choose Save Picture As to open the Save Picture dialog box, which is shown in Figure 6-9.

Figure 6-9   Saving an image.

2. Save the file.

Select a folder, a filename, and a type, and click Save.

To print a Web page you have open in Internet Explorer, simply click the Print button. By default, background colors and background images are not displayed, which saves printing time, spooling time, and cartridge ink. If you want to print background images and colors, follow these steps:

1. Open the Internet Options dialog box.

Click the Tools menu, click Internet Options, and then click the Advanced tab, which is shown in Figure 6-10.

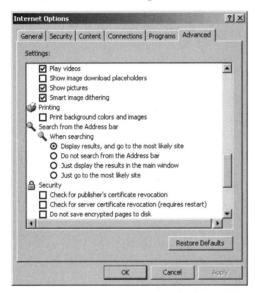

Figure 6-10   The Advanced tab in the Internet Options dialog box.

2. Enable background printing.

Scroll down the Settings list, and click the Print Background Colors And Images check box. Click OK.

To print a Web page and exercise finer control over what's printed, follow these steps:

TIP   *Although Windows 2000 ships with Internet Explorer 5.01, if you have updated your system using Windows Update you probably have Internet Explorer 5.5 or newer. Internet Explorer 5.5 and later versions contain the extremely handy Print Preview feature. To use Print Preview, choose the File menu's Print Preview command.*

1. **Open the Print dialog box.**

   Click the File menu, and then click Print. For the most part, you use this dialog box just as you would use any Print dialog box in Windows. If you have any questions, check Skill 3.

2. **Specify your options.**

   Click the Options tab, which is shown in Figure 6-11. If you want to print all pages linked to the current page, click the Print All Linked Documents check box. (Be sure that you really want to do this step—you might need lots of paper.) If you want to print a table that lists the links for this page, click the Print Table Of Links check box.

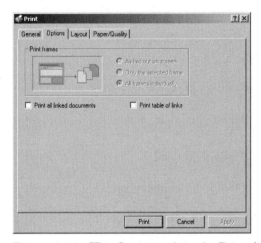

Figure 6-11   The Options tab in the Print dialog box.

3. **Print the document.**

   Click the Print button.

   To print the target of any link, right-click the link, and choose Print Target from the shortcut menu to open the Print dialog box.

Searching on the Internet

If you've spent any time at all searching the Internet, you probably know about search services such as Yahoo!, Excite, InfoSeek, AltaVista, and Lycos. You know that you can go to those sites and enter a search term or phrase to locate documents and other resources that contain references to your search item. With Internet Explorer, however, it's possible to search all those services at the same time plus a few more. You can also specify whether you want to find a Web page, a person's address, a business, a map, or a picture, for example.

Doing a simple search

Before getting into all the options you can apply to a search, do a simple search for something that all business professionals want to know from time to time: salary comparisons. Follow these steps:

1. Open the Search bar, which is shown in Figure 6-12.

Click the Search button.

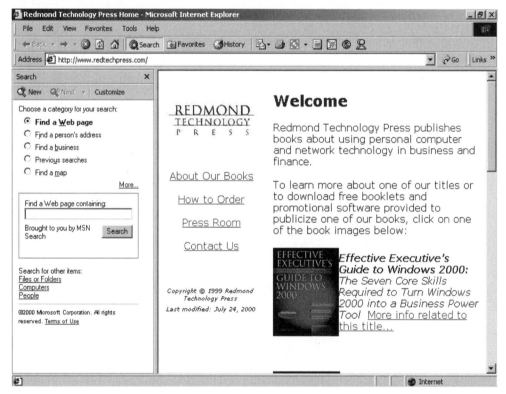

Figure 6-12   Opening the Search bar.

2. Enter a search phrase.

In the Find A Web Page Containing box, type "*salary comparisons.*" (Type the quotation marks but not the period. Using quotation marks this way indicates a search for resources that contain both words, not just one or the other.) Click Search. Figure 6-13 shows the results of my search.

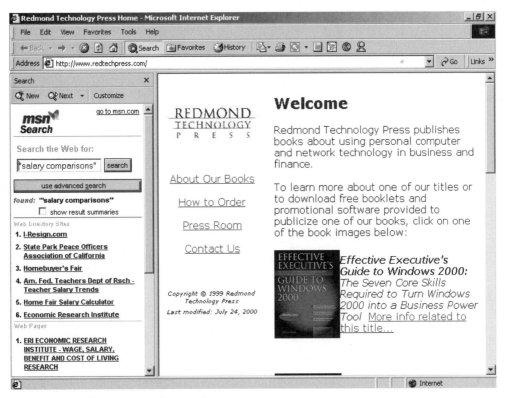

Figure 6-13 The results of a search.

To open a document, simply click it. To begin a new search, click the New button.

Broadening a search

If you want to broaden a search after you've seen the results of your first search, click the Use Advanced Search button. As Figure 6-14 shows, you'll see more options that you can use to be more specific about your search.

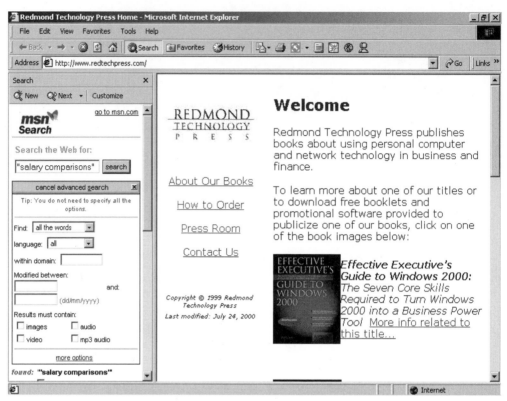

Figure 6-14   Specifying more search options.

For even more additional options, click the More Options link at the bottom of the Search bar to open MSN Search, as shown in Figure 6-15.

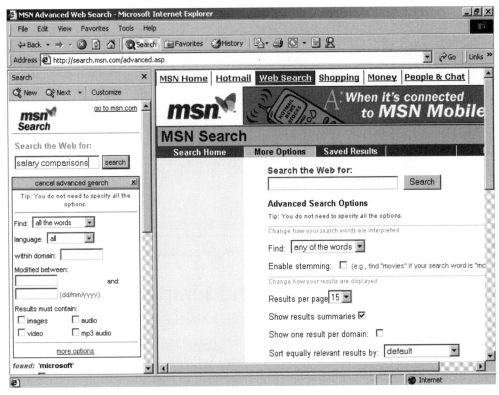

Figure 6-15 Opening MSN Search.

To further refine a search, click the Customize button to open the Customize Search Settings dialog box, which is shown in Figure 6-16. You use this dialog box to specify the search services you use to find individual items. For example, you can choose to use InfoSpace, Bigfoot, and WorldPages to find a person's mailing address, or you could specify to use only one of the three. Scroll down through this dialog box to see your other options. Notice that at the bottom of the dialog box you can check the Previous Searches check box to tell Internet Explorer to store the results of the last ten searches.

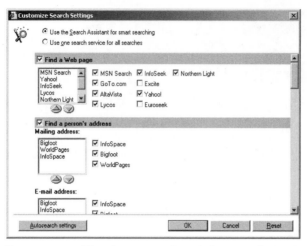

Figure 6-16 The Customize Search Settings dialog box.

Understanding cookies and temporary Internet files

A *cookie* is a file stored on your computer by the server of a site you visit. This simple data file identifies you to the server. When you revisit the site, the cookie can be used to welcome you by name or to present you with a customized version of the page. A cookie cannot see what's on your hard drive or local network, nor can it send any other information back to the server or run other programs on your computer.

A temporary Internet file is a copy of a Web page you have visited and is stored in the Temporary Internet Files folder on your hard drive, along with your cookies. When you access a site you've visited before, Internet Explorer first checks to see whether the page is in your Temporary Internet Files folder. If it is, Internet Explorer then checks to see whether the page has been updated since being stored. If the page has not been updated, Internet Explorer opens it from your Temporary Internet Files folder (also called the *cache*), which is much faster than loading the page from the server.

You can check out what has been stored in your Temporary Internet Files folder and empty it whenever you want. Follow these steps:

1. Open the Internet Options dialog box.

Click the Tools menu, and then click Internet Options.

2. Open the Settings dialog box, as shown in Figure 6-17.

Click the General tab, and then click the Settings button.

Figure 6-17   The Settings dialog box.

3. Open the Temporary Internet Files folder, as shown in Figure 6-18.

In the Settings dialog box, click the View Files button.

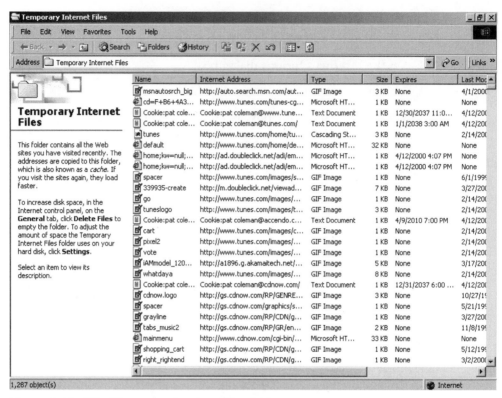

Figure 6-18   The Temporary Internet Files folder.

As you can see, the Temporary Internet Files folder contains both cookies and the URLs of Web pages stored on your computer. To empty the Temporary Internet Files folder, click the Delete Files button on the General tab in the Internet Options dialog box (note that this doesn't delete cookies). To increase or reduce the space for the Temporary Internet Files folder, move the slider bar in the Settings dialog box.

To empty the Temporary Internet Files folder automatically when you close Internet Explorer, follow these steps:

1. **Open the Internet Options dialog box.**

   In Internet Explorer, click the Tools menu, and then click Internet Options.

2. **Tell Internet Explorer to empty the folder.**

   Click the Advanced tab, scroll down to the Security section, and click the Empty Temporary Files Folder When Browser Is Closed check box. Click OK.

Managing E-Mail with Outlook Express

Outlook Express is an Internet standards e-mail reader, which means that you can use it to send and receive e-mail if you have an Internet e-mail account. An e-mail account is not the same thing as an account with an online information service such as CompuServe or America Online. An Internet e-mail account provides Internet e-mail but does not provide services such as proprietary AOL chat rooms, access to databases, or conferences, for example.

These days, most ISPs provide you with an e-mail account as well as access to the Web. Before you can use Outlook Express to send and receive e-mail, you need to configure your e-mail account using the Internet Connection Wizard by following the instructions in the first section of this skill.

Understanding the Outlook Express window

You can open Outlook Express in the following ways:

- Click the Launch Outlook Express button on the Quick Launch toolbar.

- Click the Start button, click Programs, and then click Outlook Express.

- In Internet Explorer, click the Mail button on the Standard toolbar, and then click Read Mail or Read News.

Figure 6-19 shows what you'll see when you open Outlook Express the first time.

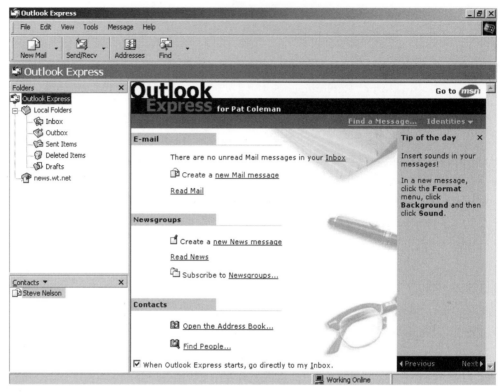

Figure 6-19 The opening screen in Outlook Express.

This window contains the usual Windows menu bar and toolbar. The Folders list is a tool for organizing messages and contains the following folders by default, although, as you will see, you can add your own folders to this list:

- The Inbox folder is the repository for newly received messages and messages you haven't disposed of in some way.

- The Outbox folder contains messages that are ready to be sent.

- The Sent Items folder contains copies of messages you have sent.

- The Deleted Items folder contains copies of messages you have deleted. In other words, unless you tell Outlook Express otherwise, messages you delete are not immediately removed but rather are placed in the Deleted Items folder.

- The Drafts folder contains messages you are working on but aren't yet ready to send.

The Contacts list contains the names of people in your Address Book. For information on how to set up and use Address Book, see Appendix A.

Reading and processing messages

From the Outlook Express main window, you can click the Inbox link or the Read Mail link to open your Inbox folder and read messages. Figure 6-20 shows the Inbox folder in Preview Pane view. Message headers appear in the upper pane, and you select a message to open it in the lower pane, or double-click a message to open it in a separate window.

TIP   *To turn off the Preview pane, click the View menu, click Layout, and in the Layout dialog box, clear the Show Preview Pane check box.*

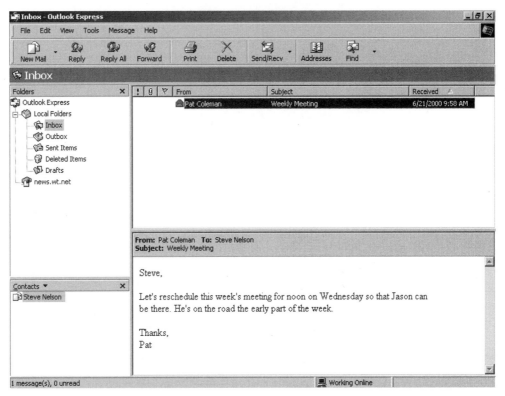

Figure 6-20   Reading a message in preview pane view.

If you are connected to the Internet, Outlook Express will automatically check the mail server for new messages and download them to your Inbox folder when you open Outlook Express. Thereafter, Outlook Express will check for new messages every 30 minutes. If you want to check for messages more often or less frequently, follow these steps:

1. **Open the Options dialog box, as shown in Figure 6-21.**

   Click the Tools menu, and then click Options.

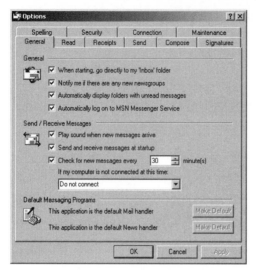

Figure 6-21   The General tab in the Options dialog box.

2. **Change the time interval.**

   On the General tab, click the Check For New Message Every *x* Minutes spin box, and select a new time period. Click OK.

By default, Outlook Express plays a sound when new messages arrive in your mailbox. If you prefer silence, clear the Play Sound When New Messages Arrive check box on the General tab of the Options dialog box.

TIP   *Use the If My Computer Is Not Connected At This Time drop-down list box on the General tab of the Options dialog box to control whether Outlook Express should automatically connect to the Internet to check your e-mail.*

Saving messages

You can save messages in Windows Explorer folders or in Outlook Express folders, and you can also save attachments to messages. We take a look at attachments later in this skill.

To save messages in Windows Explorer folders, open the message or select its header, and follow these steps:

1. Open the Save Message As dialog box, as shown in Figure 6-22.

Click the File menu, and then click Save As.

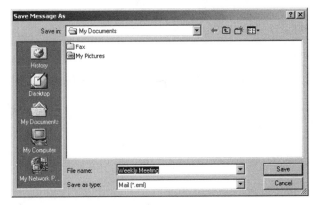

Figure 6-22 The Save Message As dialog box.

2. Select a folder.

Select a folder, and then accept the filename that's suggested, or type a new filename.

3. Select a file type.

In the Save As Type drop-down box, choose how to save the message, and then click Save.

To save a message in an Outlook Express folder, simply drag its header to the folder. You can also create your own folders. For example, you might want to create a folder for a project and then place all correspondence related to that project in that folder. Or you might want to create a folder for a person and place all messages from that person in that folder. To create a new Outlook Express folder, follow these steps:

1. Open the Create Folder dialog box, as shown in Figure 6-23.

Click the File menu, click New, and then click Folder.

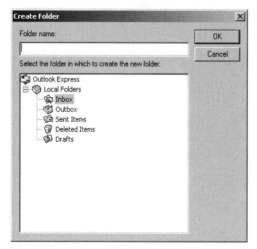

Figure 6-23   The Create Folder dialog box.

2. Name the folder.

In the Folder Name box, enter a name for the folder.

3. Select a folder in which to place the new folder.

You can place the folder as a main folder in the Local Folders list, or you can store it in any existing folder. Click OK.

Printing messages

If you need a paper copy of a message, you can print it in the following ways:

- Select the header of the message and click the Print button on the toolbar.

- Open the message, and then click the Print button in the message window.

- Select the message or open the message, click the File menu, and then click Print.

Whichever method you use, you'll open the standard Windows Print dialog box. If you have any questions about how to use this dialog box, look back at Skill 3.

Marking messages

Later in this skill are some suggestions for managing your electronic office; one suggestion is that you don't need to read and process every message as it arrives in your Inbox. When you're checking mail, you can mark messages so that when you have time you can go back and deal with them. You can mark messages in the following ways:

- To identify a message as important, select the message header, click the Message menu, and click Flag Message to place a little red flag to the left of the header.

- If you've read a message but want to read it again later and respond, you can mark it as unread. Select the message header, click the Edit menu, and then click Mark As Unread. Rather than see an open envelope preceding the header, you'll see a closed envelope, and the header is in boldface.

Replying to messages

To reply to a message from a single sender, you simply click the Reply button on the toolbar. If the message was sent to multiple recipients, you can reply to them and to the sender by clicking the Reply All button. By default, Outlook Express places all the names of those you reply to in your Address Book—a quick and easy way to store e-mail addresses.

By default, Outlook Express includes the text of the original message in your reply. Sometimes this feature can be helpful, and at other times it can be a real nuisance. You have a couple of alternatives if you don't want the original message included in the reply:

- Click the Reply button, place your cursor in the body of the message, click the Edit menu, click Select All to highlight the message, and press Delete.

- Click the Tools menu, click Options to open the Options dialog box, click the Send tab, clear the Include Message In Reply check box, and click OK. Now the message will never automatically be included in the reply.

Forwarding messages

Sometimes it's very handy to forward a message, and you can include your own comments in the forwarded message. As is the case with passing along anything created by somebody else, be sure that forwarding a message will not infringe on the original sender. Of course, some people maintain that you should never put anything in an e-mail message that you wouldn't want to see on the front page of the newspaper—but that's probably a topic for discussion at happy hour.

To forward a message, open it, click the Forward button, enter an e-mail address, add your comments if you want, and click the Send button.

Deleting messages

You can delete a message in the following ways:

- Select the message header, and press Delete.

- Open the message, and press Delete.

By default, deleted messages are placed in the Deleted Items folder, and they stay there until you manually empty the Deleted Items folder. To do so, select the Deleted Items folder, click the Edit menu, click Empty 'Deleted Items' Folder, and click Yes when you are asked whether you want to delete these items.

WARNING *When you empty the Deleted Items folder, the items are permanently deleted—they do* not *go to the Recycle Bin first.*

To automatically clear the Deleted Items folder when you close Outlook Express, follow these steps:

1. Open the Options dialog box.

Click the Tools menu, and then click Options.

2. Select the Maintenance tab, as shown in Figure 6-24.

Click the Maintenance tab, click the Empty Messages From The 'Deleted Items' Folder On Exit check box, and click OK.

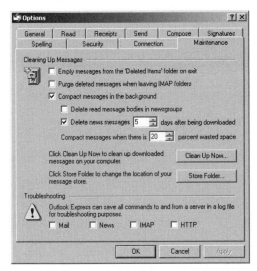

Figure 6-24 The Maintenance tab in the Options dialog box.

Creating and sending messages

You can create a message in two formats: plain text and HTML. By default, Outlook Express uses HTML. As you'll see in the next section, not all e-mail programs can deal with HTML messages, so you'll want to use that format with caution. To compose and send a message in plain text, follow these steps:

1. Open the New Message window, as shown in Figure 6-25.

Click the New Mail button on the toolbar.

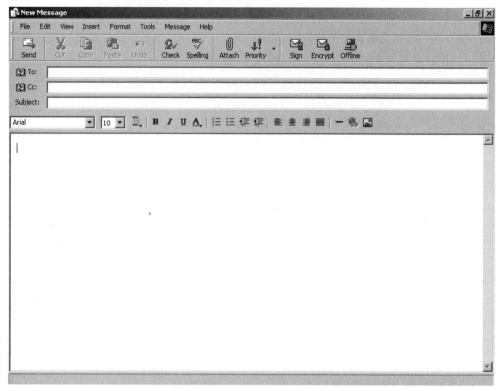

Figure 6-25 The New Message window.

2. Specify plain text format.

Click the Format menu, and choose Plain Text.

3. Address and compose your message.

On the To line, enter an e-mail address, or click the icon to open your Address Book and select the address. Follow the same procedure to copy someone on the message. To send a blind (secret) carbon copy of the message, click the Cc icon to open the Select Recipients dialog box, select a name from the list, and click the Bcc button. Enter a subject on the Subject line, place the cursor in the message body, and type your message.

4. Send the message.

Click the Send button.

By default, messages are sent immediately if you are connected to the Internet. If you want to wait and send a message later, click the File menu, and choose Send Later. This action places your message in the Outbox folder, and it is sent when you click the Send/Recv button.

Using HTML

When you use HTML to create a message, you are essentially creating a Web page, and you can include several neat effects, such as a background color or image, or sound, for example. The drawback, as mentioned earlier, is that not all e-mail programs can deal with these Web pages, including America Online and the older, freeware versions of Eudora. Before you send someone a message that includes pictures and other HTML elements, send that person a plain text message and ask whether they can read HTML messages.

When you open the New Message window and see the Formatting toolbar, as shown in Figure 6-25, you know that you're set up to compose a message in HTML. The Formatting toolbar contains many of the tools you see and use in your word processor. You can use it to do the following tasks, among other things, in your message:

- Insert a bulleted list.
- Add effects such as boldface, italics, underline, and font color.
- Insert a numbered list.
- Format paragraphs as flush left, flush right, or centered.
- Insert a horizontal line.
- Insert a picture.
- Specify a font and a font size.

Figure 6-26 shows an e-mail message that contains HTML elements.

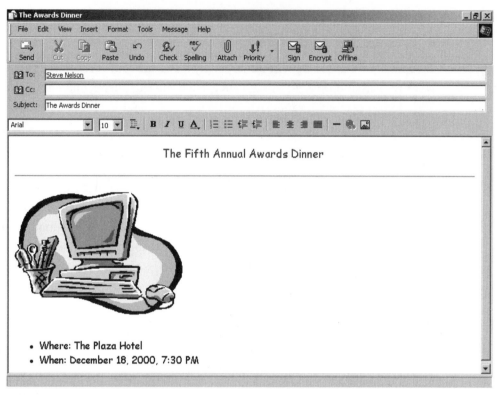

Figure 6-26 An e-mail message composed in HTML.

Using stationery

You can also liven up your messages using stationery, or you can create your own stationery. Figure 6-27 shows a message that uses the Formal Announcement stationery included with Outlook Express.

Figure 6-27 A message that uses stationery.

To use stationery, choose the Message menu's New Message Using command, and then select a stationery design from the list, or choose Select Stationery from the list to open the Select Stationery dialog box. You'll find several more designs listed in this dialog box. To create your own stationery, click the Create New button to start the Stationery Setup Wizard.

Sending files with messages

Earlier, this skill mentioned that you can save files attached to messages. Obviously, you can also attach files to messages. Before getting into the details, though, keep in mind that some rather serious computer viruses make the rounds via attachments to e-mail. Many businesses would cease to function these days if they couldn't e-mail files to colleagues and clients, so abandoning the use of file attachments is not an option. To be on the safe side, I recommend not opening an attachment if you don't know its source; just select the message header, and press the Delete key. Be particularly wary of an attachment that appears to have been forwarded several times.

NOTE *Security updates to Outlook Express available using Windows Update have reduced the risk of attachments by preventing you from opening the most dangerous types of attachments, although it's always advisable to never open unsolicited attachments and to always use a virus-checking program.*

When you receive a message that has a file attached to it, you'll see a paper-clip icon preceding the header. When you open the message, you'll see the filename of the attachment on the Attach line. If the file is in a format that a program on your computer can read, simply double-click the filename of the attachment to open it. To save the attachment, follow these steps:

1. Open the Save Attachments dialog box.

Click the File menu, and choose Save Attachments.

2. Save the file.

In the Save To box, specify a folder in which to save the file, and click Save.

To attach a file to a message you are composing, follow these steps:

1. Open the Insert Attachment dialog box, as shown in Figure 6-28.

Click the Insert menu, and choose File Attachment.

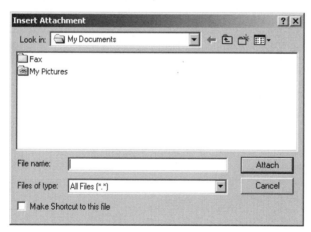

Figure 6-28   Attaching a file.

2. Attach the file.

Enter the filename in the File Name box or browse to find it, and then click Attach.

Your message now contains the name of the file on the Attach line.

Creating a signature

Many people never bother to sign their e-mail messages. After all, their name appears on the From line. Others create elaborate signatures that are automatically appended to all messages. Your business or organization might, in fact, have guidelines about what you should include in a signature. It commonly includes your name and title, the name of your organization and perhaps its physical address, and your phone number.

To create a signature that is automatically appended to all your messages, follow these steps:

1. **Open the Options dialog box and select the Signatures tab, which is shown in Figure 6-29.**

   Click the Tools menu, click Options, and then click the Signatures tab.

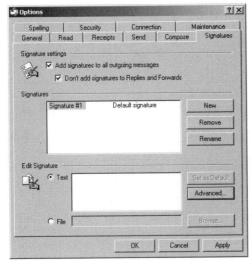

Figure 6-29   Creating a signature.

2. **Create a signature.**

   Click New, and then enter your contact information in the Text box. If you have a text of HTML file that contains the information you want in your signature, click the File option button, and click Browse to locate the file.

3. **Specify the e-mail accounts for which you'll use this signature.**

   Click the Advanced tab to open the Advanced Signature Settings dialog box. If you have a home e-mail account and a business e-mail account, for example, you might want to specify a different signature for each one. Select the account, and click OK.

4. **Specify which messages will use the signature.**

If you want the signature attached to all outgoing messages, click the corresponding check box. If you don't want the signature automatically added to all messages, leave this check box cleared. To add the signature to selected messages, click Insert in the New Message window, and then click Signature. When you have made your selections, click OK.

Filtering messages

You are not at the mercy of your Inbox. You can choose to block mail from certain senders, and you can route mail from other senders directly to a specific folder. To do any of these tasks, you use the Message Rules dialog box. Using the options in this dialog box, you can get very detailed about how you filter messages. This section looks at the steps for blocking messages entirely from certain senders and for routing messages from a particular person to a folder, but you can apply these steps to establish many other message rules.

To block messages from a particular sender, follow these steps:

1. **Open the Message Rules dialog box and select the Blocked Senders tab, which is shown in Figure 6-30.**

Click the Tools menu, click Message Rules, and then click Blocked Senders List.

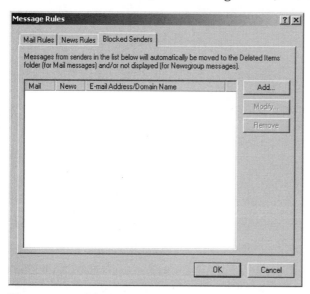

Figure 6-30 Blocking messages.

2. Open the Add Sender dialog box, which is shown in Figure 6-31.

Click the Add button in the Message Rules dialog box.

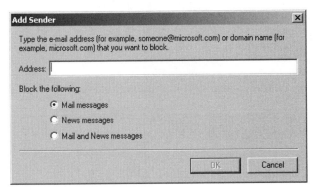

Figure 6-31 The Add Sender dialog box.

3. Specify who and what you want to block.

In the Address box, enter the e-mail address of the sender you want to block, and then select whether you want to block mail messages, news messages, or both. Click OK, and then click OK again back in the Message Rules dialog box.

Now all messages from that e-mail address will go immediately to your Deleted Items folder when they are downloaded to your system.

NOTE   *In addition to being an e-mail reader, Outlook Express is also a newsreader. Newsgroups are collections of articles (news) on specific topics, and you can access them from the news server of your ISP. For the most part, newsgroups are not particularly valuable to business professionals, so this skill does not cover them.*

To establish a rule that sends all mail from a specific person to a specific folder in Outlook Express, follow these steps:

1. Open the New Mail Rule dialog box, which is shown in Figure 6-32.

Click the Tools menu, click Message Rules, and then click Mail. If you have existing message rules, click the New button to open the New Mail Rule dialog box.

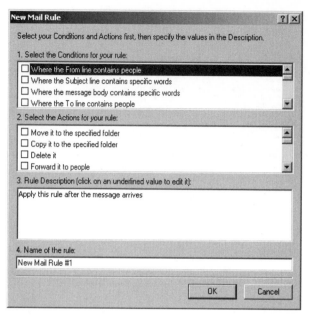

Figure 6-32   The New Mail Rule dialog box.

2. Specify the conditions and actions for your new rule.

In the Select The Conditions For Your Rule section, click the Where The From Line Contains People check box, and, in the Select The Actions For Your Rule section, click the Move It To The Specified Folder check box. You'll now see links in the Rule Description section that you can click to specify the person and the folder.

3. Specify the person.

Click the Contains People link to open the Select People dialog box, as shown in Figure 6-33. Enter the e-mail address of the person, or select it from your Address Book, and click Add.

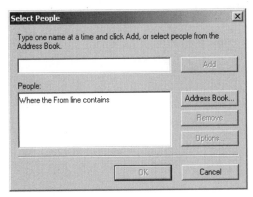

Figure 6-33   The Select People dialog box.

4. Specify the folder.

Click the Specified link to open the Move dialog box, as shown in Figure 6-34. Create a new folder, or select an existing folder, and click OK.

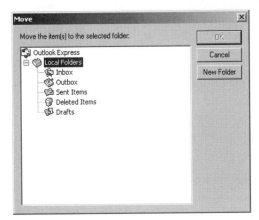

Figure 6-34   The Move dialog box.

5. Name your new rule.

Back in the New Mail Rule dialog box, enter a name in the Name Of The Rule box, and click OK.

Now all the mail from the person you specified will go immediately to that person's folder when it's downloaded to your system.

Using identities

An identity in Outlook Express is sort of an e-mail user profile. Although identities often aren't appropriate in business settings—separate user accounts work better in most cases—you can use identities if more than one person uses your Windows 2000 Professional computer and thus also uses Outlook Express. When you set up identities, each person sees only her e-mail messages and has her own contacts in Address Book.

When you install Windows 2000 Professional, you are set up as the main identity. To set up other identities, follow these steps:

1. Open the New Identity dialog box, which is shown in Figure 6-35.

In the main Outlook Express window, click the File menu, click Identities, and then click Add New Identity.

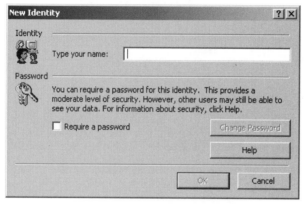

Figure 6-35 The New Identity dialog box.

2. Specify a name and, optionally, a password for this identity.

In the Type Your Name box, enter a name for the new identity. If you want password protection enabled, click the Require A Password check box, which opens the Enter Password dialog box. Type the password twice—once in the New Password box and again in the Confirm New Password box—and then click OK.

The name of the new identity will appear on the Identities list in the Manage Identities dialog box, and you'll be asked whether you want to switch to the new identity now. If not, click No, and then click Close in the Manage Identities dialog box. The first time you log on as the new identity, you'll be asked for some information about your Internet connection.

To switch from one identity to another, follow these steps:

1. Open the Switch Identities dialog box, as shown in Figure 6-36.

Click the File menu, and then click Switch Identity.

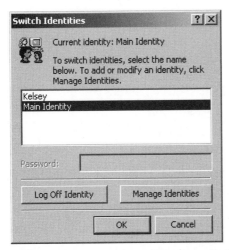

Figure 6-36 The Switch Identities dialog box.

2. Select the identity.

Select an identify from the list, enter a password if required, and click OK.

After you set up more than one identity, you'll be asked to select an identity when you open Outlook Express.

Managing Your Electronic Office

Do you ever wonder how you'd get by without the number of communications tools you now have at your disposal? Phone, voice mail, fax, e-mail, pagers, the Internet and its vast supply of instant resources—even paper memos, reports, and home-to-office network connections—the list seems endless. Or, maybe you wonder instead how to get your work done in the midst of all these tools.

A recent issue of *Harvard Management Update,* a newsletter published by the publishing arm of Harvard Business School, had some suggestions that I've adapted for inclusion here. Not every suggestion applies to all situations, but you're sure to find among them some that will help you better manage the deluge of information that faces you in your electronic office.

- You don't have to read e-mail the instant you hear the you-have-mail alert. Some business professionals set aside certain times each day to check e-mail. You don't have to be interrupted unless you want to be. If something is really urgent, the sender will probably find another way to get in touch with you.

- You don't have to answer the phone just because it rings. You can let voice mail pick it up and then respond during the day at times that let you give your full attention to the matters at hand.

- Don't open every e-mail message. If the subject line tells you that another get-rich-quick scheme has just landed in your mailbox, press the Delete key. Agree with your colleagues to use the priority symbols available in Outlook Express for things that are time sensitive.

- If an e-mail message looks interesting but you can tell that it isn't essential, print it and read it later or flag it in some way.

- Rather than use e-mail for team projects, set up an intranet (an internal Internet) or a newsgroup to which members can post messages.

- Take care of paper filing first, and then set up an electronic filing system for e-mail. Create folders for projects and people, for example, and be diligent about moving messages into these folders.

- If you have tons of old messages lying around, just get rid of them. If you can't bear that thought, save them to a file somewhere.

- When you create a new document, save it in its correct folder immediately, using the techniques discussed in Skill 2.

- Multitask. Return phone calls while printing something, or check your paper organizer while downloading a file from the Internet.

- Don't waste time by following links that have nothing to with the reason you're searching the Internet.

- Unsubscribe to newsletters you no longer need or never get around to reading.

- Regularly evaluate your sources of information—journals, periodicals, reports, and memos, for example—and discontinue all that are not essential. Be on the lookout for new information sources that will keep you current.

- Set aside 5 to 10 minutes each day to learn something new about any of your electronic tools.

Summary

This skill looked at four major topics: connecting to the Internet via a dial-up connection, browsing the Internet with Internet Explorer, using Outlook Express to send and receive e-mail, and managing an electronic office. This information is far from being everything you would ever want to know about using the Internet, so if you're new to these tools, you might want to take to heart the last suggestion in the preceding list and spend a few minutes a day fiddling around with Internet Explorer or Outlook Express.

Skill 7

PERFORM PREVENTIVE MAINTENANCE AND TROUBLESHOOTING

Featuring:

- Protecting the Health of Your Computer System
- Getting Information About Your System
- Cleaning Up Your Hard Drive
- Speeding Up File Retrieval
- Scheduling Maintenance
- Looking at System Resources
- Using the Windows 2000 Troubleshooters
- Starting Windows 2000 in Safe Mode
- Using an Emergency Repair Disk
- Using Recovery Console
- Troubleshooting Your Network

According to experts who have been running large and small networks with Windows 2000 (both Server and Professional), this operating system really is what it was cracked up to be—stable. And, as mentioned in an earlier skill, this version has been described as virtually "crashless." That doesn't mean, however, that it's maintenance free and that nothing will ever go wrong.

The first part of this skill describes some practical environmental considerations that influence the well-being of your computer system. The next part describes some tools included with Windows 2000 Professional that you can use to enhance its native stability. You can even schedule these tools to run automatically during times when your system doesn't need to be used for business purposes. The last part of this skill gives you some guidelines about what to do when something does go wrong.

Protecting the Health of Your Computer System

Although you probably know that spilling a cup of coffee on your keyboard is not a good idea, you might not know what room temperature is safe for computers. Here are some tips about the physical setup of your computer system that can prolong its life and save on repair costs:

- Excessive heat can seriously damage your system. The recommended maximum room temperature is 85 degrees F, and the minimum is 60 degrees F.

- If you're serious about protecting your data, install an uninterruptible power supply (UPS). It is basically a high-powered battery with an intelligent switch. When the power goes off, the UPS swings into action and powers the computer on the fully charged battery until the computer has time to safely shut-down.

- Keep cables and power cords routed away from high-traffic areas, and use surge protectors, which typically have one cord running to the wall outlet and space for five or six plugs. Be sure, though, that the power circuit can handle the load.

- Don't place any piece of electronic equipment in direct sunlight.

- Clean the inside and outside of your machines periodically using a can of compressed air or the blower mode of a shop vacuum. And don't forget your printer—paper dust collects quickly in a printer.

- Minimize the effects of static electricity, for example, by raising the humidity with an evaporative humidifier or adding plants or an aquarium. Static electricity can shorten the life of a computer chip, if not destroy it.

- Don't plug any heating element into the same outlet as a computer—no coffee maker or heater, for example.

Getting Information About Your System

If you're having trouble with a computer and need the help of technical personnel, you'll want to have some information at hand. Depending on the nature of the problem, you might be asked how much free space is on your hard drive, what kind of modem you have and how is it setup, or what type of video adapter is installed. The quickest way to access this information is to open the System Information dialog box, which is shown in Figure 7-1.

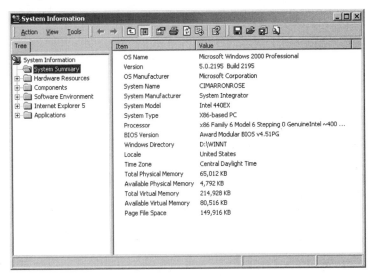

Figure 7-1　The System Information dialog box.

To open the System Information dialog box, click the Start button, click Programs, click Accessories, click System Tools, and then click System Information. What you'll see in this dialog box depends on what is installed on your computer and how it is configured. To display more information about an item, click the plus sign (+) next to the item to expand it. For example, to display information about your modem, expand the Components folder in the Tree pane, and then select Modem. Modem information is then displayed in the right pane.

Using the System Information dialog box, you can get details about every component in your system, including hardware, software, drivers, and printers, for example.

Cleaning Up Your Hard Drive

In the preceding skill, you saw how to locate and delete temporary Internet files and cookies from your system. But in the process of managing your computer, Windows 2000 Professional creates a number of other temporary files. Some speed the performance of the graphical interface, and some are for setup purposes, for example. If you're pressed for hard drive space, you'll want to be diligent about getting rid of files you no longer need. The tool you use for this task is Disk Cleanup.

To run Disk Cleanup, follow these steps:

1. **Open the Select Drive dialog box, as shown in Figure 7-2.**

   Click the Start button, click Programs, click Accessories, click System Tools, and then click Disk Cleanup.

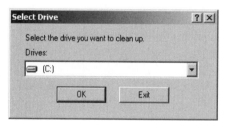

Figure 7-2   The Select Drive dialog box.

2. **Open the Disk Cleanup dialog box, as shown in Figure 7-3.**

   Select the drive you want to clean up, and then click OK. Disk Cleanup checks the selected drive and then opens the Disk Cleanup dialog box.

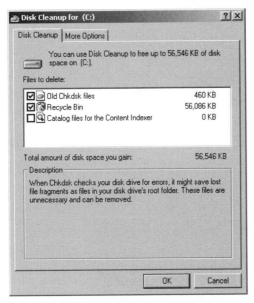

Figure 7-3　The Disk Cleanup dialog box.

3. Select the files you want to delete.

Click the check box next to the category of files you want to delete, and then click OK.

If you want to remove Windows components you don't use or programs you don't use, click the More Options tab. Clicking Cleanup in the Windows Components section starts the Windows Components Wizard, and clicking Cleanup in the Installed Programs section opens the Add/Remove Programs dialog box.

Running Disk Cleanup every two or three months is recommended. Even if you aren't pressed for hard disk space, getting rid of files that are useless is a good idea.

Speeding Up File Retrieval

When Windows 2000 Professional writes a file to your hard disk, it places the file wherever it finds room. Over time, any one file can have a piece here, a piece there, or a piece somewhere else. Windows 2000 Professional always knows the location of these pieces and can access them whenever you want to open the file, although going to several locations takes longer than if all the pieces were in one place.

To speed up file retrieval, you can run Disk Defragmenter to round up the bits and pieces and organize them so that applications can find and load the file faster. To defragment the files on your hard disk, follow these steps:

1. **Open the Disk Defragmenter dialog box, which is shown in Figure 7-4.**

   Click the Start button, click Programs, click Accessories, click System Tools, and then click Disk Defragmenter.

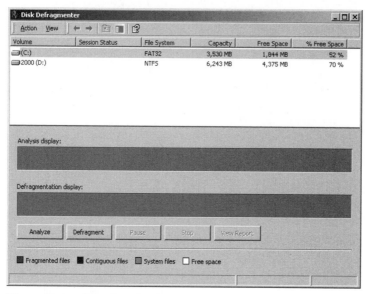

Figure 7-4   The Disk Defragmenter dialog box.

2. **Analyze the disk.**

   Select the disk, and click the Analyze button. After a few seconds, you'll see a screen similar to the one shown in Figure 7-5 and a message box that will tell you whether the drive needs to be defragmented. Notice the colored squares at the bottom of the Disk Defragmenter dialog box; the analysis display provides a graphical image of fragmented files, contiguous files, system files, and free space.

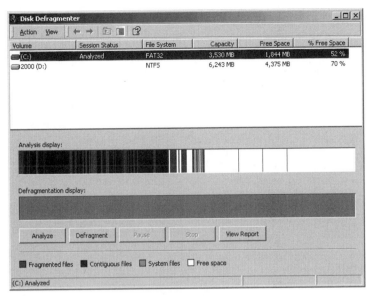

Figure 7-5   Analysis of a hard disk.

3. Get more information about the disk.

To get more information, such as the names of the fragmented files, their size, and the number of fragments, click the Action menu, and choose View Report.

4. Defragment the drive.

If both you and Windows 2000 Professional decide that defragmenting is necessary, click the Defragment button to start the process.

Defragmenting a drive can take awhile, and you can do other work during the process, although your response will be slower. Also, whenever you save a file, Disk Defragmenter will start all over again. It's best to run Disk Defragmenter at a time when you don't need to be doing anything else on your computer, and doing so about once a month should be sufficient.

Scheduling Maintenance

As the preceding section explained, you can clean up your hard drive or defragment it whenever the need arises, and you can also schedule these tasks to be taken care of automatically, perhaps after the workday or on the weekend. To schedule maintenance tasks, follow these steps:

1. **Open the Scheduled Tasks folder, which is shown in Figure 7-6.**

   Click the Start button, click Programs, click Accessories, click System Tools, and then click Scheduled Tasks.

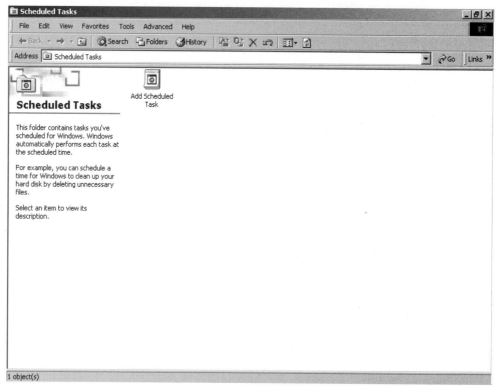

Figure 7-6   The Scheduled Tasks folder.

2. **Start the Scheduled Task Wizard.**

   Click Add Scheduled Task, and, at the opening screen of the wizard, click Next.

3. **Select a task.**

Click the application name, as shown in Figure 7-7, and click Next.

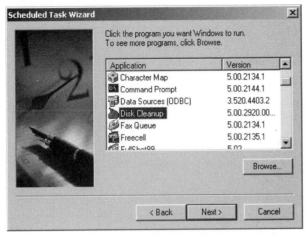

Figure 7-7   Selecting a task to schedule.

NOTE   *You can also use the Scheduled Task Wizard to specify a program that always starts when you log on to your computer.*

4. **Name the task, and select a time to run it.**

Accept the suggested name or enter another name, and then click the option button that corresponds to when you want the task to run. Click Next, and further specify the exact time and dates to run the program. Click Next.

5. **Specify a username and a password.**

Enter a username, enter a password, and confirm the password. The task will run as though that user started it.

6. **Add this task to the Scheduled Tasks folder.**

Click Finish.

To add other tasks, repeat steps 1 through 6.

Looking at System Resources

Earlier, this skill looked at a quick way to get information about your system. You can get more details using some other tools that come with Windows 2000 Professional.

Using the Performance console

The Performance console is in some ways a rather esoteric tool, although you can use it to monitor and log hundreds of system variables, including random access memory (RAM) usage, how much CPU time an application is using, and repeated failed logons. This type of information is useful in a number of ways. For example, if RAM usage is consistently high, you might want to consider installing more RAM in your computer. If a particular application is using excessive CPU time, that could explain a degradation in overall system performance. And, if you see a number of repeated failed logons, you might begin to suspect that a password-guessing program is attempting to crack your system.

To open the Performance console, click the Start button, click Settings, click Control Panel, and then click Administrative Tools to open the Administrative Tools folder. Click Performance. Figure 7-8 shows the Performance console when you first open it. The area on the right is blank until you specify what to monitor.

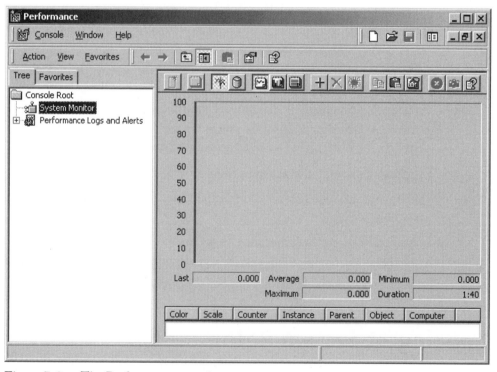

Figure 7-8   The Performance console.

The variables you monitor with the Performance console are *counters;* to specify which counter to monitor, you use the Add Counters dialog box, which is shown in Figure 7-9. To open the Add Counters dialog box, click the Add button on the toolbar (it has a plus sign on it).

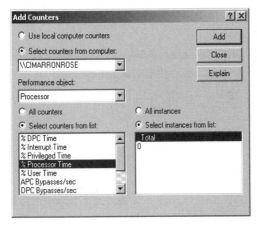

Figure 7-9   The Add Counters dialog box.

This section doesn't describe all the counters you can monitor or all of their many ramifications, although it can show you basically how to add and monitor a counter. For demonstration purposes, add a counter for the number of files that have been opened on your local computer and a counter that indicates how hard your processor is working. Open the Add Counters dialog box, and then follow these steps:

1. **Select a performance object.**

   The subsystem components of Windows 2000 Professional are classified into objects, and each object has counters. On the Performance Object drop-down list, select Server.

2. **Select a counter.**

   Click the Select Counters From List option, and then select Files Opened Total. To see a description of this counter, click the Explain button. Close the explanation, and then click Add.

3. **Add another object and a counter.**

   On the Performance Object drop-down list, select Processor, and then, in the Select Counters From List box, select %Processor Time. Click Add, and then click Close.

Back on the Performance console, you'll see a graphical display of the counters you've just added. By default, information is displayed in Chart view. If you want a report instead, click the View Report button (it's a little notebook). If you want a bar chart, click the View Histogram button (it shows a little bar chart).

Using Task Manager

Another colorful way to display information about your system is to use Task Manager. You can open Task Manager in the following ways:

- Right-click an empty area of the taskbar, and choose Task Manager from the shortcut menu.

- Click the Start button, click Run to open the Run dialog box, and type *taskmgr* in the Open box.

- Press Ctrl+Alt+Del to open the Windows Security dialog box, and click the Task Manager button.

The Windows Task Manager dialog box opens with the Performance tab selected, as shown in Figure 7-10.

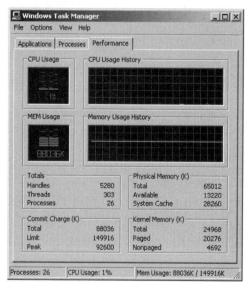

Figure 7-10   The Performance tab in Windows Task Manager.

The two top boxes display in graphical form CPU and memory usage. The lower boxes give you numeric information about your system. Click the Applications tab to find out which applications are running on your system. If you want to close an application, select it, and click the End Task button. Click the Processes tab to see a list of all currently running processes, how long each has been running, and how much memory each is using, for example.

Using Event Viewer

If you're having trouble with a computer, your first line of defense might be to use the Windows Troubleshooters, which is discussed next, depending on the way in which the computer is misbehaving. A very useful way to peek inside your Windows 2000 Professional system is to open Event Viewer, which displays event logs.

To open Event Viewer, click the Start button, click Settings, click Control Panel, click Administrative Tools, and then click Event Viewer. Figure 7-11 shows the Event Viewer window.

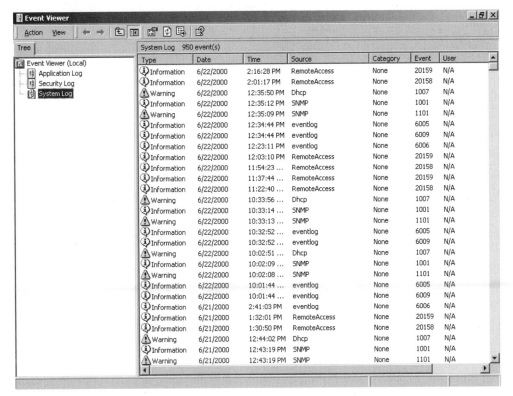

Figure 7-11 The Event Viewer window.

When you start Windows 2000 Professional, Event Viewer begins to track events and stores them in three logs:

- The Application Log contains events that applications generate. The developer of the application specifies which events to log. Any user can take a look at the Application Log.

- The Security Log contains information such as failed logon attempts and successful and failed audits. Only an administrator can view the Security Log, and the administrator can specify which events are logged in the Security Log.

- The System Log contains events logged by Windows 2000 Professional components. For example, if a device driver fails to load, that event will be noted in the System Log. Any user can view the System Log.

To view a log's contents, select it in the Tree pane. To view details about a particular event, right-click it, and choose Properties from the shortcut menu to display the event's Properties dialog box. Figure 7-12 shows the Properties dialog box for an error event in the Application Log.

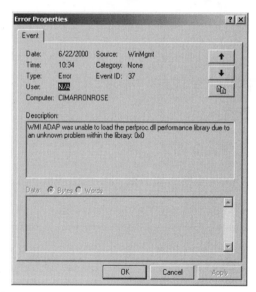

Figure 7-12 The Properties dialog box for an error event.

The Application and System Logs track three types of events:

- An Information event is identified by the letter *i* in a bubble, which indicates that the event was successfully completed.

- A Warning event is identified by an exclamation point in a yellow triangle, which indicates that a condition is not yet crucial but could be in the future.

- An Error event is identified by a white X in a red circle, which indicates a problem.

The Security Log tracks successful and failed events. A successful event is identified by a yellow key, and a failed event is identified by a yellow lock.

Although you can specify which events are logged only if you are an administrator and only for the Security Log, you can specify the maximum size of the log file, how long to keep events in the log file, and which events are displayed for any log. Follow these steps:

1. Open the Properties dialog box for a log.

Right-click the log in the Tree pane, and choose Properties from the shortcut menu. Figure 7-13 shows the Application Log Properties dialog box.

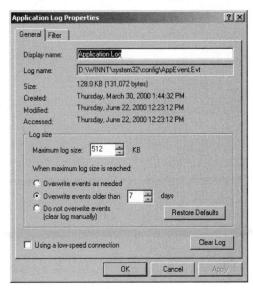

Figure 7-13   The Application Log Properties dialog box.

2. **Specify the log size.**

In the Maximum Log Size spin box, select a size.

3. **Specify whether and when to overwrite events that have been logged.**

In the When Maximum Log Size Is Reached section, click an option button.

4. **Specify which events to display.**

Click the Filter tab, and clear the check box for the type of event you don't want displayed. This step can be helpful when you want to see only error events, for example. You can use the other options in this dialog box to specify the event source, the category, the event ID, the user, the computer, and a time period. When you've made your selections, click OK.

Using the Windows 2000 Troubleshooters

Now that you have looked at how to get information about your system, you can look at your options when you realize that something is wrong. Don't neglect the Windows Troubleshooters, which walk you through a series of steps for solving problems with your modem, your printer, your monitor, a camera, or a scanner, for example. What you get for free with the Troubleshooters is suggestions and advice that in the past you would get when you called Microsoft Technical Support—and that isn't free.

Other skills mentioned that you should click the Troubleshoot button if you're having difficulty with something. For example, when you set up a printer and the test page doesn't print correctly, click the Troubleshoot button to start the Print troubleshooter.

To display a list of Troubleshooters, follow these steps:

1. **Open Help.**

Click the Start button, and then click Help.

2. **Locate the Windows 2000 Troubleshooters topic.**

Click the Contents tab, expand Troubleshooting And Maintenance, and then click Windows 2000 Troubleshooters. You'll see the list shown in Figure 7-14.

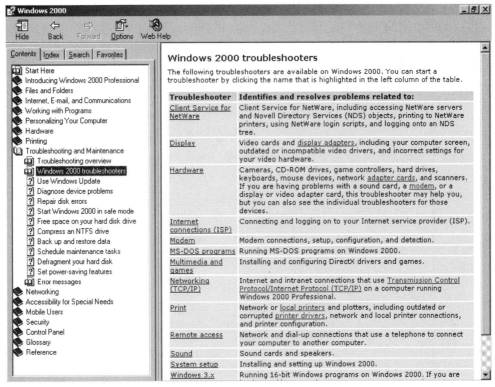

Figure 7-14 Displaying a list of Windows 2000 Troubleshooters.

To start a Troubleshooter, click its link in the Troubleshooter column. It's usually helpful to keep the Troubleshooter steps on the screen, so click the Hide button to display only the right portion of this window. To display the tabs again, click Show.

To see how a Troubleshooter works, suppose that you're having a monitor problem—the screen flickers. Follow these steps:

1. Open the Display Troubleshooter, which is shown in Figure 7-15.

On the list of Troubleshooters, click the Display link.

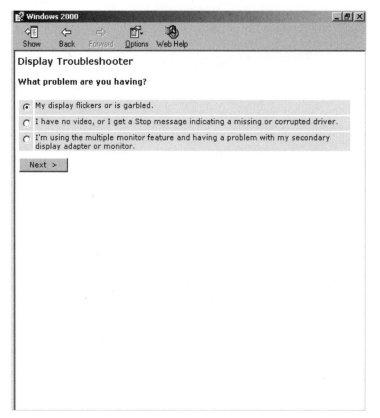

Figure 7-15 Starting the Display Troubleshooter.

2. Describe the problem.

Click the My Display Flickers Or Is Garbled option, and click Next.

3. Follow the onscreen instructions and answer the questions.

On the next screen are some ideas about what to try or adjust. If those don't work, click the option indicating that you still have a problem, and click Next. Continue until you've solved the problem or completed the Troubleshooter.

The Troubleshooters certainly will not solve every problem that arises with your Windows 2000 Professional system, although they are an excellent place to start. At the very least, you'll have much more information about what is working and what is not working than you did to start with. To get additional help, go to Microsoft's Support Online site at support.microsoft.com—there you can query the Microsoft Knowledge Base—the same database of technical articles Microsoft Technical Support uses when you call for help.

Starting Windows 2000 in Safe Mode

If you're having a problem the Troubleshooters can't solve, your next step might be starting Windows 2000 Professional in Safe mode. Figure 7-16 shows the desktop in Safe mode.

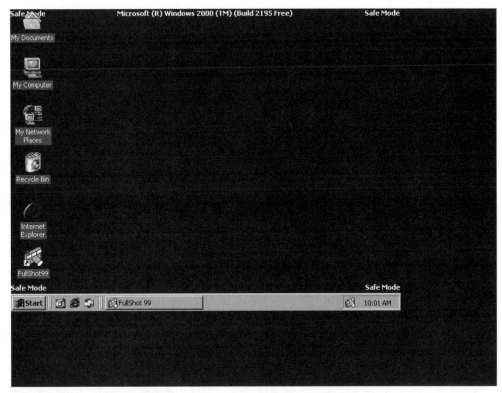

Figure 7-16   The Windows 2000 Professional desktop in Safe mode.

Typically, you use Safe mode if you install a new application or a new driver for a device and Windows 2000 Professional won't start. In Safe mode, you can remove the offending application or driver and even reinstall the operating system if that becomes necessary. To start Windows 2000 Professional in Safe mode, press F8 when you see the bars at the bottom of the screen when Windows 2000 Professional tries to start up. You can then use the arrow keys to select from the following options on the Windows 2000 Advanced Options menu:

- Safe Mode uses only a minimal set of device drivers and services, including the mouse, the keyboard, hard drive, basic video, and default system services. Safe mode does not use any network connections.

- Safe Mode With Networking loads the basic drivers and the network drivers.

- Safe Mode With Command Prompt loads basic drivers and opens Windows 2000 Professional at a command prompt rather than on the desktop.

- Enable Boot Logging saves information about which drivers were or were not loaded in a text file (nbtlog.txt). You can open this file in Notepad and look for the cause of your startup problem.

- Enable VGA Mode starts the system using a basic VGA driver. If you load a new video driver that causes problems, you won't be able to see enough information on the screen to perform even basic tasks. Restart the computer in VGA mode.

- Last Known Good Configuration starts Windows 2000 Professional using the Registry information that was saved when you last shut down.

- Directory Services Restore Mode is available only for Windows 2000 domain controllers.

- Debugging Mode starts Windows 2000 Professional and sends debugging information through a serial cable to another computer. This very specialized option might be used by system administrators in specific circumstances.

- Boot Normally restarts Windows 2000 Professional in regular mode.

- Return To OS Choices Menu displays the menu from which you choose an operating system if you have a system that dual-boots Windows 2000 Professional and another operating system.

After you select an option, be patient. Eventually, though, you will see the Log On dialog box, and Windows 2000 Professional will open in the mode you selected. To return to regular mode, if you can, restart the system.

Using an Emergency Repair Disk

If nothing suggested in this skill works, the next tool in your troubleshooting bag of tricks is the emergency repair disk. Haven't made one yet? Follow these steps:

1. Open the Backup program.

Click the Start button, click Programs, click Accessories, click System Tools, and then click Backup.

2. Open the Emergency Repair Diskette dialog box, as shown in Figure 7-17.

In the Backup dialog box, click the Emergency Repair Disk icon.

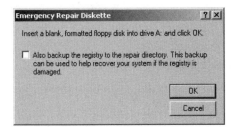

Figure 7-17 The Emergency Repair Diskette dialog box.

3. Insert the floppy.

Insert the floppy disk in its drive, click the check box to specify that the information is also backed up to the Repair folder, and then click OK. A bar indicates the progress of the copy.

WARNING *The Repair folder is stored in the WINNT folder. Don't change the contents of this folder or remove it.*

4. Store the ERD in a safe place.

Label and date the disk, and put it in a safe place where you can find it when you need it.

To use the ERD to repair your system, boot the system using the four Windows 2000 Setup disks or your installation CD, and then follow these steps:

1. **Choose the Repair option.**

   When Setup asks whether you want to continue with the installation, press Enter, and then press R to run the repair process using the ERD.

2. **Choose the repair type.**

   You have two choices: Fast and Manual. Fast Repair works quickly without your intervention and tries to repair the Registry, system files, and the boot sector. Fast Repair uses a backup copy of the Registry that was created when you first ran Setup on your machine. Manual Repair lets you choose whether to repair system files and the boot sector, but does not let you repair the Registry. You have to use Recovery Console to repair the Registry. (Recovery Console is covered in the next section.) Unless you are a very advanced user, choose Fast Repair.

3. **Begin the repair process.**

   Be sure that your installation CD and your ERD are handy. Follow the instructions on the screen, and insert one or the other when asked to do so.

If the repair process is successful, you are set. Your computer will restart automatically. If the repair process is not successful and you are an advanced user, you can use Recovery Console.

Using Recovery Console

To use Recovery Console, you must be logged on as an administrator, and you should be well versed in the inner workings of Windows 2000 Professional. Recovery Console is run from the command prompt. To use the Recovery Console, follow these steps:

1. **Boot with the Setup Disks or CD.**

   Boot the system using the four Windows 2000 Setup disks or your installation CD.

2. **Launch the Recovery Console.**

   When Setup asks whether you want to continue with the installation, press Enter. After this, press R, and then press C to start the Recovery Console. Specify which Windows 2000 installation you want to repair, then enter the password for the local Administrator account (the password you entered when you *first* installed Windows 2000). To use the Recovery Console, you use a limited set of administrative commands. To display a list of these commands, type *help* at the command prompt.

Troubleshooting Your Network

Troubleshooting a network can be complicated if the network is large and sprawling and involves miles of cables and all sorts of peripherals. Troubleshooting even a small network can be complicated, although you can try a handful of things that will often solve the most straightforward problems.

First, ask yourself or others on your network some questions:

- Is this problem happening on only one computer or on all computers on the network?

- Does the problem occur all the time or only intermittently?

- Can you or the user reproduce the problem?

- Has the function ever worked? If so, when did it stop working? What were you doing at the time?

Answering these questions can help you determine whether the problem is isolated or networkwide or if it always happens or is a random event (the most difficult to troubleshoot). If you can reproduce the problem, you have a good chance of tracking down its source. If the function has never worked (for example, connecting to the network), you might suspect a malfunctioning network card. If you can figure out what was happening when the problem began, you also have a good chance of tracking down the source. If you ask and answer these questions and you still don't have a clue, try the following suggestions.

Checking out My Network Places

If you suspect that your computer is not communicating with other computers on the network, open My Network Places (click its icon on the desktop). If you see at least one other network computer, you can rather safely assume that your network card and cabling are okay.

Checking out Event Viewer

As you know from an earlier section in this skill, you can use Event Viewer to troubleshoot. Take a look in the Application, Security, and System Logs for error events (they're preceded by an X in a red circle). Right-click an event, and choose Properties from the shortcut menu to open the Properties dialog box for an event, which describes the error in detail. Figure 7-19 shows the Properties dialog box for an error event in the Application Log on my system.

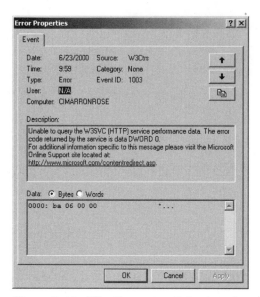

Figure 7-19   The Properties dialog box for an error event.

TIP   *The cause of a problem could be occurring at startup. To find out, try this tech-nique: Reboot the system, notice the time, and then check Event Viewer for any errors reported at that time.*

Checking out Device Manager

To take a look at Device Manager, right-click My Computer, choose Manage from the shortcut menu, expand System Tools in the Computer Management window, and click Device Manager. Right-click any device that's preceded by a yellow exclamation point, which indicates a problem with the device. You'll see the status of the device and an explanation of any problem with it.

Paying attention to the status area

As you might remember, the status area is on the far right end of the taskbar. An offline icon in the status area could mean that your network card is disconnected. Check to see that the cable is connected to the card and that the card is properly seated.

Verifying computer protocols

If you have a peer-to-peer network, you are probably using the NetBEUI protocol, as Skill 4 described. If you have a client/server network, you might be using TCP/IP. Regardless of which type of network you have, all the computers on the network should be using the same protocol. To check this out, follow these steps on each computer:

1. **Open the Network And Dial-Up Connections folder.**

   Click the Start button, click Settings, click Control Panel, and then click Network And Dial-Up Connections.

2. **Open the Local Area Connection Properties dialog box, as shown in Figure 7-20.**

   Right-click Local Area Connection, and choose Properties from the shortcut menu.

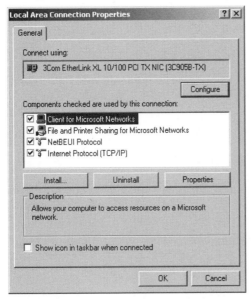

Figure 7-20 The Local Area Connection Properties dialog box.

Verify that the same protocol is checked on each computer.

Summary

Business professionals know that a portion of every day—sometimes a major portion—involves solving problems. You can minimize this problem-solving time as it concerns your network or computer system by using the preventive maintenance suggestions in the first part of this skill. When the inevitable happens, though, you can begin the troubleshooting process by using the tools described in the last part of this skill. If that doesn't solve your problem, you'll need to acquire the services of a technician. In the worst case, you'll have to reinstall Windows 2000 Professional, although you have a number of things to try before facing that prospect. And don't forget that your best insurance is an up-to-date backup of your system and your data files, as you learned in Skill 2.

Appendix A

REVIEWING THE WINDOWS 2000 PROFESSIONAL ACCESSORIES

Featuring:

- Creating an Address Book
- Using NetMeeting
- Using the Windows 2000 Word Processors
- Sending and Receiving Faxes
- Using Calculator

Earlier in this book, you learned that an *applet* is a small application and that the items in Control Panel are referred to as applets. Windows 2000 Professional comes with a number of other small applications called accessories, and you'll find them on the Accessories menu (click the Start button, click Programs, and then click Accessories). This skill discusses only those accessories that are useful in a business situation. Others, such as System Tools, have been discussed in the skills in the main part of this book. For information about the others—such as Games, Entertainment, and Paint—look in Windows 2000 Professional Help.

Creating an Address Book

Skill 6 showed that an easy way to enter an e-mail address in Outlook Express is to add it from your Address Book. This section gives you an overview of Address Book and shows you how to set it up to quickly locate contact information and to set up group, or distribution, lists.

You can open Address Book in a couple of ways:

- From the desktop, click the Start button, click Programs, click Accessories, and click Address Book.

- In Outlook Express, click the Addresses button on the toolbar in the main window or click the To: button in the New Message window (which opens the Select Recipients dialog box in Address Book).

Figure A-1 shows an empty Address Book window, ready for you to add contact information. Notice that this Address Book is for the main identity. (See Skill 6 for details about identities.)

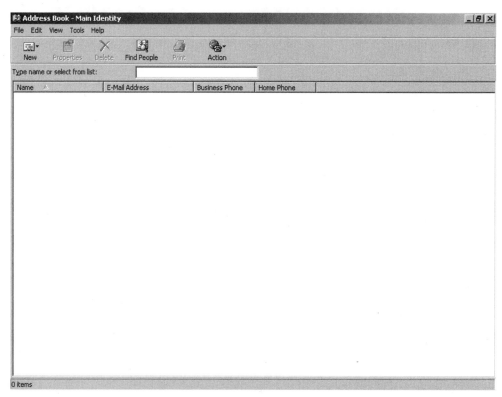

Figure A-1   An empty Address Book window.

Adding information for an individual

To add contact information for an individual, open the Address Book and follow these steps:

1. Open the Properties dialog box, as shown in Figure A-2.

Click the New button on the toolbar, and then click New Contact.

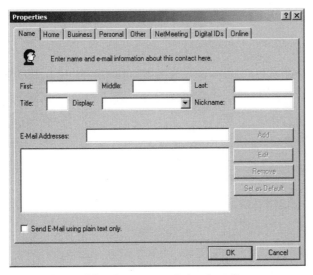

Figure A-2   The Properties dialog box for a new contact.

2. Add information for this person.

Use the Name, Home, Business, Personal, Other, NetMeeting, Digital IDs, and Online tabs to add as much or as little information as you want. Press the Tab key to move from one field to another in a tab.

NOTE   *You'll see the Online tab only if you have MSN Messenger installed and the contact you created is a member of your MSN Messenger contacts list, which is discussed in the next section.*

3. Close the Properties dialog box.

Click the Close button. You'll see the new contact listed in the Address Book window. To send mail to this new contact, click the To: button in the New Message window, double-click the name, and click OK.

Setting up a distribution list

In Address Book, a distribution list is called a *group*. To set up a group, follow these steps:

1. Open the Properties dialog box for the new group, which is shown in Figure A-3.

In Address Book, click the New button on the toolbar, and then click New Group.

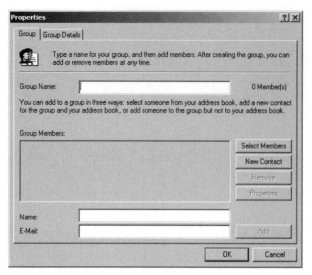

Figure A-3 The Properties dialog box for a new group.

2. Name the group.

In the Group Name box, type a name for the book. This name will appear on the list in the main Address Book window.

3. Add members to the group.

You can add members in the following ways:

- Click the Select Members button to open the Select Group Members dialog box, select a name from the list, and click OK.

- Click New Contact to open the Properties dialog box for a new contact, enter contact information, and click OK to add a member to the group and to your Address Book.

- In the Name and E-Mail fields at the bottom of the window, enter informa tion to add someone to the group but not to your Address Book.

When you're finished, click OK.

The group name now appears in boldface in the main Address Book window.

Locating people

Using Address Book, you can find contact information for people by using directory services such as Yahoo! People Search, Bigfoot Internet Directory Service, and WhoWhere Internet Directory Service if you are connected to the Internet. To do so, follow these steps:

1. **Open the Find People dialog box, as shown in Figure A-4.**

   In Address Book, click the Find People button on the toolbar.

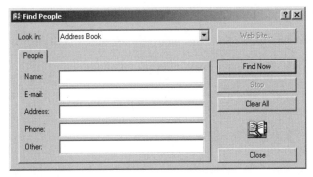

Figure A-4   The Find People dialog box.

2. **Select a directory service.**

   Click the Look In drop-down list box.

3. **Enter some information.**

   Fill in the information you know about this person, and then click Find Now. If you get too many results, add more information; if you get too few, try searching only on the last name.

Printing your Address Book

You can print the contents of your Address Book in three formats:

- Memo, which prints all the information you have stored.

- Business Card, which prints the information you typically find on a business card.

- Phone List, which prints only the phone numbers.

To print in one of these formats, click the Print button to open the Print dialog box, select a print style (Memo, Business Card, or Phone List), and click Print.

Creating and printing a map

If your organization is having an offsite retreat, if you're inviting your employees for dinner at your new house, or if you just need directions to a business meeting, you can use Address Book to create and print a map to the location. Follow these steps:

1. Open the Properties dialog box.

In the Address Book window, right-click an entry in your Address Book, and choose Properties from the shortcut menu.

2. Enter an address.

Click either the Home or Business tab. You can use the address that's stored for the person's name you clicked, or you can simply enter other address information for the map you want to produce. When you're done, click View map. This displays a map of the location in Internet Explorer, as shown in Figure A-5 (you may be prompted to provide some additional information first).

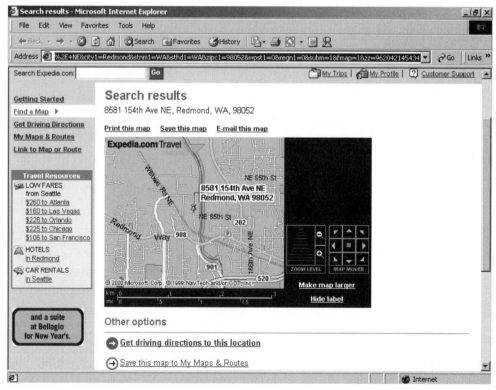

Figure A-5   Creating a map with Address Book.

You can print this map, save it, or e-mail it to someone, just like any other Web page.

Using NetMeeting

You can use the NetMeeting application to do the following if you have the proper equipment:

- Chat with someone over the Internet using the telephone or by typing on the screen

- Hold an audioconference

- Hold a videoconference

- Share applications

- Collaborate on documents

- Transfer files

- Draw on the whiteboard

To open NetMeeting, click the Start button, click Programs, click Accessories, click Communications, and then click NetMeeting. Figure A-6 shows the main NetMeeting window. Place the mouse cursor over a button to display a ScreenTip that describes what the button does.

Figure A-6   The main NetMeeting window.

Before you can use NetMeeting, you need to configure it. To do so, open NetMeeting and follow the onscreen instructions.

Placing a call

To use NetMeeting to make a call, both the sender and the receiver need microphones, sound cards, and speakers. To place a call, follow these steps:

1. Open the Place A Call dialog box, as shown in Figure A-7.

In the NetMeeting main window, click the Place Call button.

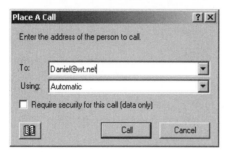

Figure A-7 The Place A Call dialog box.

2. Enter an address.

In the To box, enter a name, an e-mail address, a computer name, a computer IP address, or a telephone number.

TIP   *In order to successfully place a call, the person you're calling needs to be running NetMeeting at the time. There are ways of making NetMeeting to telephone calls, but this requires a special gateway that most users won't have access to.*

3. Place the call.

Click Call.

Chatting on the screen

After you are connected to another computer, you can also use the other NetMeeting applications, such as Chat. Figure A-8 shows the Chat window. To open it, click the Chat button in the main NetMeeting window.

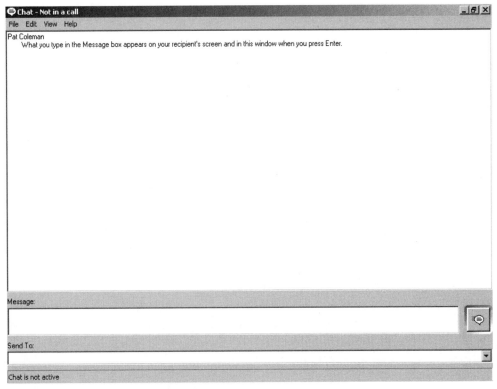

Figure A-8 Using Chat in NetMeeting.

To use Chat, you need to know only the following:

- To communicate, type in the Message box, and press Enter.

- If a Chat session involves more than you and one other person, click the down arrow in the Send To box to specify whether to send the message to the whole group or to only one person.

- To save the contents of a Chat session, click the File menu, and then click Save As.

- To end a Chat session, click Close.

Using the other NetMeeting applications

For particulars on the other NetMeeting applications, look in Windows 2000 Professional Help. The following list describes, in general, what each one does and any special equipment you need in order to use it:

- Click the Find Someone In A Directory button to use directory servers. A directory server is maintained by an organization, and when you log on to it, you can see information, such as names and e-mail addresses, of others who are logged on. Click a name to communicate with that person.

- To host a meeting over NetMeeting, click the Call menu, and then click Host Meeting to open the Host A Meeting dialog box. You can start a meeting, place outgoing calls, accept incoming calls, share a document, use the whiteboard, chat, and transfer files.

- If you have a camera attached to your computer, you can send video, and, of course, you can videoconference if you have a camera and sound equipment. You can, however, receive video even if you don't have a camera. To configure your video camera with NetMeeting, click the Tools menu, click Options to open the Options dialog box, and then click the Video tab.

- To share applications in a meeting, open the application you want to share, click the Share Program button to open the Sharing dialog box, select the program you want to share, and then click the Share button.

- If you are in a call or in a meeting, you can transfer files. Click the Transfer Files button to open the File Transfer dialog box, click Add File to select a file, click the name of the person to send the file to, and click Send All.

Using the Windows 2000 Word Processors

Windows 2000 Professional comes with two word-processing applications: Notepad and WordPad. If you've used any other word processor, you'll find that using either Notepad or WordPad is extremely easy. Therefore, rather than show you step by step how to create a document, save a document, open a document, and so on, this section will give you an overview of what each word processor is best used for and describe the basic differences between the two word processors.

To open either Notepad or WordPad, click the Start button, click Programs, click Accessories, and then click either Notepad or WordPad. Notepad is a simple text editor, and WordPad is a simple word processor. To produce complicated documents of any length, you'll want to use a fully featured word processor, such as Microsoft Word.

Before getting into details about Notepad, consider this reminder: When you open a Web page in Internet Explorer and look at its HTML source code, the document opens in Notepad. Figure A-9 shows the underlying HTML source code, open in Notepad, for the home page of Redmond Technology Press.

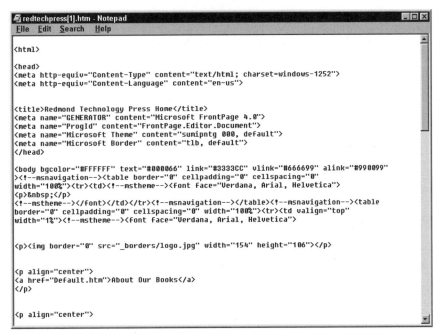

Figure A-9 The underlying HTML for a Web page open in Notepad.

Although many excellent applications are available for creating Web pages, many experts prefer to create Web pages by hand—that is, by entering the HTML code itself directly in a text editor. And Notepad is a good choice for this purpose. Notepad saves documents as pure text files, without any formatting information. Formatting information that is included in an HTML document might not appear when the page is opened in a Web browser and might even produce errors.

Usually, you use Notepad to display the contents of the Clipboard, program files, ReadMe files, and some system files. On the other hand, you can use WordPad to create and format documents and to send a WordPad document as an attachment to an e-mail message. If you've used other word processors, the WordPad window, as shown in Figure A-10, will look familiar. Place the mouse cursor over a button to display a ScreenTip that describes what the button does.

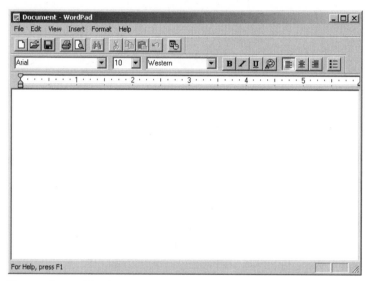

Figure A-10 The WordPad window.

To send a WordPad document as an attachment to an e-mail message, follow these steps:

1. Open the New Message window in Outlook Express.

Create or open a document in WordPad, click the File menu, and then click Send.

2. Address and send the document.

Address the document, enter a subject line, type a message if you want, and click Send.

A copy of the message is placed in your Outbox in Outlook Express. To send it immediately, open Outlook Express, connect to the Internet, and click Send/Recv.

Sending and Receiving Faxes

To send and receive faxes at your Windows 2000 Professional computer, you need a fax modem. A fax modem can be used to connect to the Internet and to send and receive faxes. If you acquired your computer within the past couple of years, you probably do have a fax modem. To verify that this is the case, open the Printers folder (click the Start button, click Settings, and then click Printers). If you see a Fax icon, your modem is a fax modem.

NOTE   *You cannot share a fax printer without additional software.*

Setting the fax service for the first time

When you installed Windows 2000 Professional, the operating system detected your fax modem, installed the fax service, and installed the associated printer. The first time you use the fax service, though, you need to do some configuration. You can fax a document from any Windows application that includes a Print menu. To set the fax service for the first time, open WordPad and follow these steps:

1. **Open a document.**

   Create a document or open an existing document to fax.

2. **Open the Print dialog box.**

   Click the File menu, and then click Print.

3. **Click to display the Fax Options tab, as shown in Figure A-11.**

   Click the Fax icon, and then click the Fax Options tab.

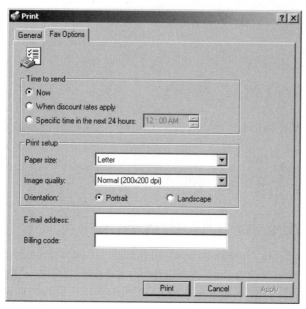

Figure A-11 The Fax Options tab in the Print dialog box.

4. Start the Send Fax Wizard.

Click the Print button. On the Welcome screen, click Next.

5. Enter the recipient and dialing information.

Fill in the To, Fax Number, and dialing rules information, and click Next.

6. Enter information for your cover page.

On the Adding A Cover Page screen in the wizard, specify whether you want to include a cover page and, if so, what it should contain. Use the Cover Page Template drop-down list box to select a type of cover page. When you're done, click Next.

7. Specify when to send the fax.

Click an option button, and click Next. At the summary screen, click Finish.

You can track the progress of the fax using the Fax Monitor dialog box, which now appears on your screen.

Receiving a fax

To set up your fax service to receive a fax, log on as an administrator and follow these steps:

1. **Open the Fax Service Management dialog box, as shown in Figure A-12.**

   Click the Start button, click Programs, click Accessories, click Communications, click Fax, and then click Fax Service Management.

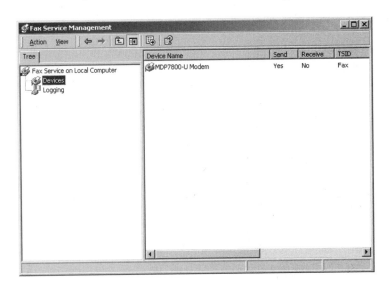

Figure A-12 The Fax Service Management dialog box.

2. **Display the name of your fax modem.**

   On the Tree pane, click Devices.

3. **Set up your fax modem to receive.**

   In the Receive column, right-click No, choose Receive from the shortcut menu to display Yes in the Receive column, and then close the Fax Service Management dialog box.

NOTE   *You can also set up fax service using the Fax applet in Control Panel. If you want to be notified when you receive a fax, open the Fax Properties dialog box (click the Fax icon in Control Panel), click the Status Monitor, and then click the Play A Sound check box.*

Using Calculator

The Calculator accessory is simply an onscreen version of the handheld variety. To open Calculator, click the Start button, click Programs, click Accessories, and then click Calculator. Calculator is available in two versions: Standard and Scientific. Figure A-13 shows Calculator in Standard view, and Figure A-14 shows Calculator in Scientific view. To change the view, click the View menu, and then select a view. When you open Calculator, it is displayed in the view you last selected before closing Calculator.

Figure A-13 Calculator in Standard view.

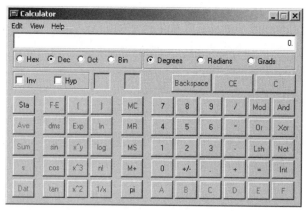

Figure A-14 Calculator in Scientific view.

In both Standard and Scientific views, Calculator has these keys:

- + represents the addition operator, – represents the subtraction operator.
- * represents the multiplication operator, / represents the division operator (+).
- Backspace erases a single digit.
- CE clears the last entry. You could press the Delete key instead.
- C clears the calculation completely. You could press the Escape key instead.
- MC clears a number from memory.
- MR recalls a number from memory.
- MS stores a number in memory and removes anything that was there already.
- M+ adds a number to the number in memory.

In Scientific view, Calculator has additional keys. To use Calculator, you simply use the mouse to click the keys you would press using the handheld variety. Or you can press the numbers at the top of the keyboard or press Num Lock and press the keys on the numeric keypad.

Appendix B

USING WINDOWS 2000 PROFESSIONAL ON A PORTABLE COMPUTER

Featuring:

- Docking and Undocking
- Conserving Battery Life
- Remote Computing

If you will be using Windows 2000 Professional on a portable computer, you will benefit by understanding three topics not discussed in the earlier chapters: docking, conserving battery life, and remote computing. This appendix briefly discusses these topics.

Docking and Undocking

If you have a portable computer that you regularly use at the office and at home or on the road, you probably know about docking stations and docking and undocking. When you're using Windows 2000 Professional, you don't need to shut down or restart your computer when docking or undocking. You do need to let the operating system know that you are about to undock your portable computer, and to do so, you use the Add/Remove Hardware Wizard. Here are the steps:

1. **Start the Add/Remove Hardware Wizard.**

   Click the Start button, click Settings, click Control Panel, and then click the Add/Remove Hardware Wizard.

2. **Tell the wizard that you are about to undock.**

   At the Welcome screen, click Next. In the Choose A Hardware Task screen, click the Uninstall/Unplug A Device option, and click Next.

3. **Tell the wizard that you want to temporarily unplug your portable.**

In the Choose A Removal Task screen, click the Unplug/Eject A Device option, and click Next.

4. **Specify that you are unplugging your portable computer.**

In the Select Device To Unplug screen, select your portable computer in the Hardware Devices list, and then click Next. When you see a message that it is safe to do so, you can undock your portable.

NOTE   *A docking station consists of a monitor and other peripherals, such as a keyboard, that you plug a portable computer into. The portable then resembles a desktop computer. A docking station is also known as a docking bay and a port replicator.*

Conserving Battery Life

If you've just undocked your portable computer, it is now running on battery power, which is great because you can now use it on the train going home, while lounging on your back deck, during a cross-country airline flight, and in other situations where an electric power source is not available. You'll find out soon enough, if you don't know already, though, that batteries don't last very long. Fortunately, you can use the power management features of your portable computer and Windows 2000 Professional to conserve battery power.

Windows 2000 Professional supports Advanced Configuration and Power Interface (ACPI), which is an industry standard that is designed to direct power management on a portable computer, on desktop computers, and also on server computers and peripherals that are ACPI-compliant. To access ACPI features, you use the Power Options applet in Control Panel. When you click Power Options, you open the Power Options Properties dialog box, which is shown in Figure B-1.

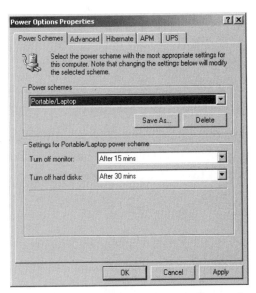

Figure B-1   The Power Options Properties dialog box.

The tabs and the options displayed in this dialog box depend on the hardware configuration of your portable computer. A power scheme is a group of options that describe your power settings. To define a power scheme, click the Power Schemes tab, if necessary, and follow these steps:

1. **Specify the type of computer you are using.**

   In the Power Schemes drop-down list box, select Portable/Laptop.

2. **Specify the idle time before a power scheme goes into effect.**

   In the Settings For Portable/Laptop Power Scheme section, select the idle time period after which the monitor is turned off and the idle time period after which your hard disk is turned off. If your system supports standby and hibernation, you will also see settings for System Standby and System Hibernates. Click Apply if you want to specify further options; otherwise, click OK.

NOTE   *In Standby, the computer goes into a low power state, from which it can quickly be restored just as you left it. In Hibernation, the computer stores the system state to the hard disk, and the computer completely shuts down. When power is restored, you can resume working exactly where you left off.*

If your portable computer has an alarm feature, you'll see an Alarms tab on which you can set a warning alarm that will alert you when your battery is low. Drag the slider to specify how low the battery should get before sounding the alarm.

You may also have a Power Meter tab in the Power Options Properties dialog box. You can check the condition of the battery charge using this tab.

Typically, the Advanced tab has only a couple of options. If you click the Always Show Icon On The Taskbar check box, a battery icon is displayed on the Taskbar. Point to this icon to display the remaining battery time. Click the Prompt For Password When Computer Goes Off Standby check box if you want to require a password before starting the computer.

Click the Hibernate tab, and then click the Enable Hibernate Support check box to enable hibernation if your computer supports that feature.

If your portable computer supports Advanced Power Management (APM)—a power management standard that ACPI replaces—simply click the APM tab to enable this feature.

Remote Computing

Skill 4 discussed how to set up your modem to dial in to a corporate network. When you're using your portable computer on the road, for example, when staying in a motel or connecting from a client's site, you may want to establish different dialing rules than those that apply in your home location. You can also set up your system to use a calling card.

Changing the dialing rules

To change the dialing rules so that you can dial out from a new location, follow these steps:

1. **Open the Phone And Modem Options dialog box, as shown in Figure B-2.**

   Click the Start button, click Settings, click Control Panel, and then click Phone And Modem Options.

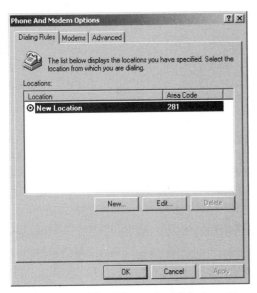

Figure B-2 The Phone And Modem Options dialog box.

2. Add a new location or edit an existing location.

Click New to open the New Location dialog box, or click Edit to open the Edit Location dialog box. The options are identical in both dialog boxes. Figure B-3 shows the New Location dialog box.

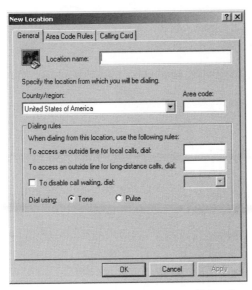

Figure B-3 The New Location dialog box.

3. **Identify the location.**

In the Location Name box, enter a name for the location. In the Country/Region section, specify the appropriate country, which determines the correct country code. In the Area Code box, enter the area code from which you will be dialing.

4. **Specify the dialing rules.**

If you need to dial a number to reach an outside line (such as 9), enter that number in the first text box. If you need to dial an additional number to access long distance service, enter that number in the second text box. To disable call waiting, select that check box, and enter the correct numeric code. You'll find it in the local phone directory. Specify tone or pulse dialing, and then click Apply.

If you're in an area that uses 10-digit dialing for local calls, you'll need to separate long distance from local calling. You do this by creating a new area code rule. Click the Area Code Rules tab in the New Location (or Edit Location) dialog box, and follow these steps:

1. **Open the New Area Code Rule dialog box, which is shown in Figure B-4.**

Click the New button.

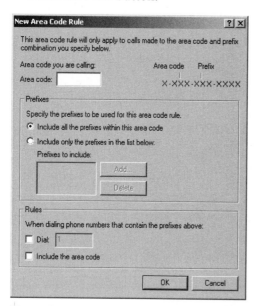

Figure B-4   The New Area Code Rule dialog box.

2. **Specify the dialing rules.**

In the Area Code box, enter the area code you will be calling. In the Prefixes section, specify what to do about prefixes. In the Rules section, specify whether to use the country code (1, which is for the United States, is the default) and whether to include the area code when dialing any prefix in the list. Click OK.

Setting up a calling card

A calling card is a handy device when you're traveling, especially if you will be billing expenses back to your employer. If you are using a calling card that is in common use and thus is listed in the Calling Card tab, click the Calling Card tab, and then follow these steps to set it up.

1. **Specify the card type.**

   In the Calling Card tab, which is shown in Figure B-5, select the card from the Card Types list.

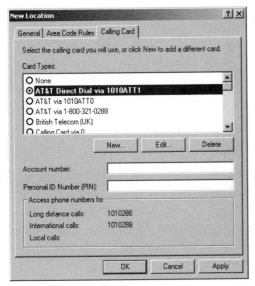

Figure B-5   The Calling Card tab in the New Location dialog box.

2. **Enter the information about your card.**

   Enter your account number, and then enter your PIN number. Access numbers are entered automatically when you select the card type. Click OK.

If your card is not listed in the Card Types list, follow these steps:

1. **Open the New Calling Card dialog box, which is shown in Figure B-6.**

   In the Calling Card tab, click New.

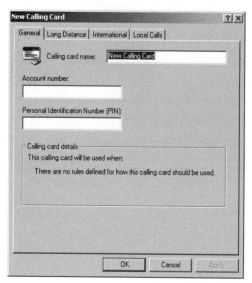

Figure B-6   The New Calling Card dialog box.

2. Enter information about the card.

In the Calling Card Name box, enter a name for the card, and then enter the account number and your PIN number.

3. Enter the steps you must follow to make a call.

Click the Long Distance tab, enter the access number, and then in the Calling Card Dialing Steps box, enter the numbers in the exact order that you must enter them to make a call. For example, click the Access Number button, press the Wait For Prompt button, click the PIN button, press the Wait For Prompt button again, and then click the Destination Number button. To change the order of a step, click the Move Up or Move Down button. Click OK.

To use your calling card to make international or local calls, click the corresponding tab, and follow step 3 above.

GLOSSARY

Accessibility Options

Features that can be used to customize Windows 2000 Professional so that it is easier to use for people who have visual, mobility, hearing, cognitive, or language impairments.

Active Desktop

A feature that, when enabled, makes your **desktop** look and work like a Web page.

Administrator

A type of **user** account in Windows 2000 Professional that has total authority over the system.

APM

An abbreviation for *a*dvanced *p*ower *m*anagement, a recently obsolete standard that extends battery life on laptop computers by shutting down components after a period of inactivity.

application

A program designed for a specific task; for example, a word processor or a database.

attachment

A file that travels along with an e-mail message.

backup

An up-to-date copy of the files on your system.

Backup Operators

A group account that contains members who can **log on** to the system, back up and restore the system, and shut down the system.

boot

The process of starting or restarting a computer system.

bus topology

A network in which all the computers are connected to a single cable line.

client/server network

A network in which one or more computers manages user accounts and resources and supplies them to the other computers. All the other computers are connected to this central computer.

command prompt

A character or a group of characters (for example, C:\WINDOWS>) on the screen that appear in a window in Windows 2000 Professional. You can enter a command at a command prompt.

cookie

A file stored on your computer by the server of a site you visit. A cookie is a data file that identifies you to the server.

desktop

The screen you see after you log on to Windows 2000 Professional. Sometimes the desktop is called a shell.

device

Any hardware peripheral that can send and receive information; for example, a printer, **modem**, or CD-ROM drive.

device driver

A program that lets a device communicate with the computer.

Disk Cleanup

A system tool you can use to identify and delete files you no longer need.

Disk Defragmenter

A system tool you can use to rearrange into contiguous units files that have become broken up into discontinuous sections on your hard drive. Using a disk defragmenter can greatly improve hard drive speed.

domain

The description of a single computer, department, or complete network that is used for administrative and naming purposes.

drive map

To assign a drive letter to represent a file, **folder**, or drive on the network. The resource then appears as though it is local to your computer.

encryption

The encoding of information so that unauthorized persons cannot access it.

ERD

An acronym for *e*mergency *r*epair *d*isk, a disk you can use to repair your Windows 2000 system.

Ethernet

The most popular networking protocol in use today.

Event Viewer

A tool that displays event logs and indicates any problem that occurs with an event.

FAT

An abbreviation for File Allocation Table, the default file system used by DOS, Windows 3.x, and the first release of Windows 95.

FAT32

An abbreviation for File Allocation Table 32, the default file system for Windows 95 release 2, Windows 98, and Windows Me.

file system

The overall structure in an operating system that determines how files are named, stored, and organized.

folder

The container for files on your system. In earlier versions of Windows and in some other operating systems, a folder is called a directory.

group account

An account that contains **user** and group accounts that share common privileges.

guest

An account on a computer or a network that has limited access and that, for security purposes, should generally not be used.

HTML

An abbreviation for HyperText Markup Language, the programming language used to create Web pages.

HTTP

An abbreviation for Hypertext Transfer Protocol, the rules that specify how a **Web browser** and a Web server communicate.

hub

The central device that connects all the computers in an **Ethernet** network.

identity

In **Outlook Express**, a type of mail user profile you can set up if multiple people use your computer and, thus, Outlook Express.

Internet

The world's largest computer network, connecting tens of millions of **users**.

Internet Explorer

The **Web browser** that's included with Windows 2000 Professional.

Internet service provider

Abbreviated as ISP; an organization that provides dedicated or dial-up access to the **Internet**.

intranet

A private corporate network that uses **Internet** technology.

IP address

A unique number that identifies a computer on a network or on the **Internet**.

ISDN

An abbreviation for Integrated Services Digital Network, a digital connection that is available through the telephone company and that can be considerably faster than a **modem** connection.

link

Short for hyperlink. A word, a phrase, an image, or a symbol that forms a connection with a resource that can be located on your local computer, your local network, or the **Internet**.

local area network

Abbreviated as LAN; a group of connected computers and other devices, such as a printer, that can share files, **applications**, and other resources.

local printer

A printer that is physically attached to your computer by a cable.

log off

To sign off on a network or a computer.

log on

To identify yourself to a network or to a computer.

magnifier

A program that displays a magnified portion of your screen in a separate window.

message rule

A filter you can apply to block mail from certain senders and route mail to specific **folders**.

modem

A device that lets you transmit and receive information to and from other computers using a telephone line.

narrator

A program that reads aloud the textual contents of the screen.

NetBEUI

An abbreviation for NetBIOS Extended User Interface, a protocol that is suitable for small, **peer-to-peer networks**.

network printer

A printer that is attached to another computer on your network, or attached directly to the network.

network topology

The physical design of a network.

newsgroup

A collection of articles on specific topics that you can access from the news server of your **Internet service provider**.

NIC

An acronym for *n*etwork *i*nterface *c*ard, an adapter that allows your computer to communicate on a local network or on the **Internet** via DSL or a cable **modem**.

NTFS

An acronym for New Technology File System, the file system supported by Windows NT and Windows 2000 Professional.

object

Any component of Windows 2000 Professional.

offline file

A file that is stored on the network but that you make available to you while you're not connected to the network.

onscreen keyboard

A keyboard that is displayed on the screen and on which you can type by clicking keys with the mouse.

Outlook Express

The news and mail reader included with Windows 2000 Professional.

password

A combination of characters you enter during the process of **logging on**.

peer-to-peer network

A network in which all computers are equals. Each computer has its own hard drive and can see and communicate with all other computers on the network. In addition, each computer can share its resources.

performance console

A tool you can use to monitor and log system variables.

permissions

The rights assigned to **user** accounts. You need permission, for example, to change the system date and time.

personalized menu

A menu that displays only the commands you most often use. Personalized menus are a Windows 2000 Professional feature that you can enable or disable.

Plug and Play

A feature of Windows 2000 Professional that automatically configures a new piece of hardware when you install it in your computer.

port

The interface through which information passes between a computer and a device such as a printer or a **modem**.

power user

A group whose members can share files and printers, change the system time, and force a shutdown of the system.

print server

A computer that shares one or more network printers with other computers on the network.

properties

Characteristics of an object or a device.

protocol

A formal specification that defines the rules whereby data is transmitted and received.

Quick Launch toolbar

The left portion of the **taskbar** that contains icons for launching programs such as Internet Explorer and **Outlook Express** and for minimizing all open windows and displaying the **desktop**.

Recovery Console

A program that advanced **users** can run to attempt to repair a system.

Recycle Bin

The container that holds deleted items until they are permanently deleted from your system.

Registry

A database that contains all the configuration information about your system.

right-click

To use the right mouse button rather than the left. You can right-click almost anywhere in Windows 2000 Professional and find useful commands.

Safe mode

A configuration in which you can start Windows 2000 Professional if it won't boot otherwise and attempt to locate the source of the problem.

screen resolution

The number of pixels on the screen. Some typical resolutions are 640 x 480, 800 x 600, and 1024 x 768.

screen saver

A utility that displays a specified image on the screen after the computer has been idle for a certain amount of time. Originally, screen savers prevented images from being permanently etched on the monitor's screen. Today's monitors need no such protection.

search service

A program that can search a file, a database, or the **Internet** for keywords and retrieve resources in which those words are found.

security

Operating system controls that limit user access. Security is one of the more important features in Windows 2000 Professional.

separator page

A page that prints between each print job on a network printer and makes it easier for **users** to identify their documents.

server

A network computer that provides services, for example, printing, storage, and communications.

sharing

Making a resource available to others on the network.

shortcut

An icon on the **desktop** that represents an **application,** a file, a document, a printer, or any other object in Windows 2000 Professional.

shortcut menu

A menu of related commands that appears when you **right-click** an **object**; also sometimes referred to as a context menu or a right-click menu.

signature

In **Outlook Express**, a text file you can append to the close of your e-mail messages. A typical business signature contains your name and title, the name of your organization and perhaps its physical address, and your phone number.

star topology

A network in which all the computers are connected to a central hub like the points of a star.

status area

The area at the far right end of the **taskbar** that contains, by default, the volume icon and the clock.

Task Manager

A tool you can use to display information about your system and to close frozen **applications**.

taskbar

The toolbar at the bottom of the **desktop** that contains icons you can use to quickly access programs.

TCP/IP

An abbreviation for Transmission Control Protocol/Internet Protocol, a set of communication protocols best suited to large networks, including the **Internet**.

temporary Internet file

A copy of a Web page you have visited and that is stored in the Temporary Internet Files folder on your hard drive.

Troubleshooter

A tool included with Windows 2000 Professional Help that you can use to solve problems with various devices, such as printers, **modems**, and network adapters.

UPS

An abbreviation for *u*ninterruptible *p*ower *s*upply, a battery source of power that swings into action when your computer loses power, such as in a brownout.

URL

An abbreviation for Uniform Resource Locator, an address for a resource on the **Internet**.

user

Any person allowed to access a computer or a network.

user account

Identifies a **user** on a network or on a computer by his or her username and password.

user profile

A collection of settings that are applied each time you **log on** to the system.

virus

A program that can attach itself to your computer system without your knowledge or permission. While not all viruses are malevolent, many are.

VPN

An abbreviation for Virtual Private Network, a tunnel through the **Internet** that securely connects your computer to your corporate network.

wallpaper

A graphical image that serves as a background on your **desktop**.

Web

Short for the World Wide Web. The most popular portion of the **Internet** consisting of myriad Web sites made up of linked Web pages containing text, images, and other elements.

Web browser

A program you can use to explore the **Web**.

Webcast

An audio or video broadcast you can tune in to and listen to over the **Internet**.

wizard

A component that steps you through a process, such as setting up a network connection or connecting to the **Internet**.

Index

E

.edu domain type, 167

electronic offices, tips for managing, 207–8

e-mail, managing with Outlook Express, 187–207. *See also* messages, e-mail

emergency repair disks, 231–32, 265

encryption, 265

ERD. *See* emergency repair disks

Ethernet, 265

event logs
  Application Log, 224, 225
  Security Log, 224, 225
  System Log, 224, 225

Event Viewer
  glossary definition, 266
  how it works, 224
  opening, 223–24
  specifying log properties, 225–26
  using to troubleshoot, 233–34
  viewing log contents, 224–25

extensions, filename, 39

F

FAT32 file system, 33, 266

FAT file system, 33, 266

Favorites list
  adding Help topics to, 15
  adding to Start menu, 29
  adding Web sites to, 171–73
  organizing, 173
  overview, 171

faxes
  receiving, 249, 251
  sending, 249
  setting up service, 249–50

File Allocation Table (FAT), 33, 266

File And Printer Sharing for Microsoft Networks protocol, 96

filename extensions, 39

files. *See also* documents
  attaching to e-mail messages, 199–200, 248
  backing up manually, 57–59
  backing up using Backup Wizard, 55–56
  backup overview, 54–55
  copying, 40–43
  creating, 39–40
  deleting, 43–44
  finding, 12–13, 44–47
  hidden, 42
  moving, 40–43
  naming, 39, 40
  offline, 50, 53–54
  opening, 35
  printing, 69–74
  renaming, 43
  restoring, 59–60
  searching for, 12–13, 44–47
  viewing types, 53
  where to store, 36

file systems
  defined, 32
  FAT, 33
  FAT32, 33
  glossary definition, 266
  NTFS, 33–34
  tips for choosing, 34
  types of, 32, 33–34

File Transfer Protocol (FTP), 167

file types, 53

filtering e-mail messages, 202–5

FilterKeys feature, 132

Find command. *See* Search command, Start menu

finding
  files and folders, 12–13, 44–47
  Internet resources using search services, 179–84
  people using Address Book, 241

Folder Options applet, 50–54, 130–31

Folder Options dialog box. *See* Folder Options applet

V

Virtual Private Networks (VPNs), 124–26, 274
viruses, 60–61, 274
visual impairment. *See* accessibility options
Volume Control dialog box, 18
Volume icon, 18
VPNs (Virtual Private Networks), 124–26, 274

W

wallpaper
  choosing, 142
  glossary definition, 274
  vs. patterned backgrounds, 140
Web, glossary definition, 275
Web browser, glossary definition, 275. *See also*
  Internet Explorer
Webcasts, 175–76, 275
Web pages
  displaying folder contents as, 51–52
  printing, 178–79
  saving, 176–78
  sending to others, 174–75
  turning on Web view, 130–31
Web view *vs.* classic Windows view, 51, 130–31
What's This? boxes, 9
wildcard characters, 46
Windows 2000 Professional
  accessibility options, 132–38
  adding and removing components, 155
  customizing, 127–61
  desktop overview, 1–29
  logging on, 2–3
  need for password, 2, 3
  vs. other Windows versions, 2, 28–29, 119
  starting in Safe mode, 229–30
Windows Explorer
  copying files and folders, 41–42
  creating files, 39–40
  creating folders, 36–37
  customizing, 50–54
  moving files and folders, 41–42

opening, 34–35
  opening files and folders from, 35
  organizing documents in, 34–47
  overview, 31–32
  Send To command, 42–43
  specifying options, 50–54
Windows Installer, 155
Windows Task Manager, 222–23
Windows Troubleshooters
  displaying list, 226–27
  glossary definition, 274
  overview, 226
  starting, 227
  using, 227–28
Windows Update site, 5–6
wizards
  Accessibility Wizard, 134–35
  Add Printer Wizard, 65–67, 105–6
  Add/Remove Hardware Wizard, 29, 152–53
  Backup Wizard, 55–56
  Create Shortcut Wizard, 27
  glossary definition, 275
  Internet Connection Wizard, 164–65
  Network Connection Wizard, 122–24, 125–26
  Offline Files Wizard, 50
  Restore Wizard, 60
  Scheduled Tasks Wizard, 218–19
WordPad
  attaching documents to e-mail messages, 248
  changing fonts, 86–87
  creating folders in, 37–39
  opening, 247
  printing files, 71–73
  when to use, 248
Write permission, 49

The manuscript for this book was prepared and submitted to Redmond Technology Press in electronic form. Text files were prepared using Microsoft Word 2000. Pages were composed using PageMaker 6.5 for Windows, with text in Frutiger and Caslon. Composed files were delivered to the printer as electronic prepress files.

Interior Design

Stefan Knorr

Project Editors

Becky Whitney
Paula Thurman

Technical Editor

Jason Gerend

Indexer

Julie Kawabata

Layout

Janaya Carter

ARE YOU A BUSINESS USER OF EXCEL 2000 OR EXCEL '97?

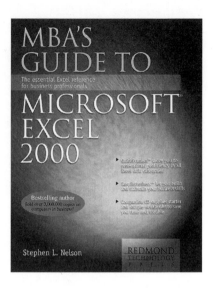

MBA's Guide to Microsoft Excel 2000: The essential Excel reference for business professionals is the only book that specifically describes how you can more easily, more productively and more powerfully use Microsoft® Excel 2000 in business.

QuickPrimers™ move you to professional proficiency in all Excel skill categories. The *MBA's Guide to Microsoft Excel 2000* begins at the beginning. If you need it, you first get friendly help on all the basics, including building simple worksheets and creating charts you can use for both analysis and presentation. If you don't need this help, you can easily skip it.

Step-by-step approach makes even Excel's most powerful tools easy to use. Once you've become comfortable with Excel, *MBA's Guide to Microsoft Excel 2000* moves you beyond the basics. You get easy-to-understand, jargon-free help on using all of Excel's business tools including PivotTables, PivotCharts, Solver, BackSolver, and Small Business Manager.

EasyRefreshers™ let you build and maintain your business skills. As you advance, *MBA's Guide to Microsoft Excel 2000* moves on and describes how to use Excel's often poorly documented tools for statistical analysis, financial calculations, sharing corporate data, and optimization modeling. Discussions usually start with *EasyRefreshers™* that let you update old skills or acquire new core business skills.

Works for all business users. Written for anyone who wants to use Excel as a business tool for powering better business decisions, *MBA's Guide to Microsoft Excel 2000* works for MBA students, MBA graduates, Excel users with undergraduate degrees in business or a related field—and for anyone else who's serious about using Excel as a tool for making better business decisions.

Companion CD supplies starter and sample workbooks. The *MBA's Guide to Microsoft Excel 2000* companion CD supplies starter Excel workbooks for business planning, profit-volume-cost analysis, break-even calculations, capital investment budgeting, asset depreciation and debt amortization so you get a head start on creating your own workbooks. The CD also supplies samples of all the workbooks discussed in the book.

496 pages, paperback, $39.95   Available at bookstores everywhere and at all online bookstores.
ISBN 0-9672981-0-5

ARE YOU AN EXECUTIVE USER OF THE INTERNET WHO NEEDS TO GET STARTED QUICKLY?

Written specifically for busy executives, managers, and other professionals, *Effective Executive's Guide to the Internet* provides a fast-paced, executive summary of the seven core skills you need to know to use the Internet at work, on the road, or at home:

Skill 1: Understanding the Environment. This skill gives you an overview of the Internet: what it is, how it works, and how it came to be.

Skill 2: Making Internet Connections. This skill provides step-by-step instructions for connecting your computer or network to the Internet.

Skill 3: Browsing the Web. This skill focuses on the Internet Explorer Web browser included with all the latest versions of Windows. We explain how a Web browser works and how to customize Internet Explorer.

Skill 4: Communicating with Electronic Mail. In this skill, we describe how to use Outlook Express, the mail and news reader included with Windows.

Skill 5: Using Search Services. This skill describes in detail how search services work and you can best use them. A special topic at the end of this skill gives you some ways to get started gathering business information.

Skill 6: Understanding Other Internet Services. In this skill, we look at FTP, Telnet, Mailing lists, and using your computer as a fax machine and telephone.

Skill 7: Publishing on the Web. Learn how Web pages work, how to develop a Web strategy, how to set up your domain and your server, how to collect and create digital content, and how to create your Web page.

ABOUT THE AUTHORS:

Pat Coleman writes about intranets, the Internet, and Microsoft Windows 2000. Formerly the editorial director of Microsoft Press, Coleman is also the co-author of the best-selling *Effective Executive's Guide to Project 2000* and *Effective Executive's Guide to Windows 2000,* both published by Redmond Technology Press.

Stephen L. Nelson: With more than 3 million books sold in English, Nelson is arguably the best-selling author writing about using computers in business. Formerly a senior consultant with Arthur Andersen & Co., he is also the co-author of *Effective Executive's Guide to Project 2000* and *Effective Executive's Guide to PowerPoint 2000.*

288 pages, paperback, $24.95   Available at bookstores everywhere and at all online bookstores.
ISBN 0-9672981-7-2

DO YOU NEED TO GET YOUR PROJECT STARTED QUICKLY?

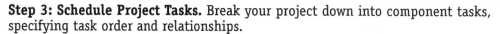

Written specifically for busy executives and project managers, *Effective Executives— Guide to Project 2000* walks you through the eight steps of organizing, managing and finishing your project using Microsoft® Project 2000:

Step 1: Learn the Language. Start here with a refresher on the language of project management and Project 2000.

Step 2: Describe the Project. Describe your project in general terms, including start date, end date and calendar of workdays.

Step 3: Schedule Project Tasks. Break your project down into component tasks, specifying task order and relationships.

Step 4: Identify and Assign Project Resources. Identify and then allocate project resources, such as people and equipment.

Step 5: Review Project Organization. Review your project for structural soundness and reasonableness.

Step 6: Present Project to Stakeholders. Present your plan to project team members and management.

Step 7: Manage Project Progress. Monitor progress and costs, assuring your project stays on course.

Step 8: Communicate Project Status. As the project progresses, keep project team members and other stakeholders apprised of the project's status and communicate important project information and changes.

ABOUT THE AUTHORS:

With more than 3,000,000 books sold in English, **Stephen L. Nelson** is arguably the best-selling author writing about using computers in business. Nelson's project management experience includes work in software development, commercial real estate development and book publishing.

Pat Coleman is a technical editor and author who writes about intranets, the Internet, Windows, and Windows applications. The co-author of *Mastering Intranets, Mastering Internet Explorer 4,* and *Windows 2000 Professional: In Record Time* (all published by SYBEX), Coleman has worked as the editorial director of Microsoft Press, deputy editor at World Almanac and as a project analyst at Encyclopaedia Britannica.

Kaarin Dolliver is the managing editor of Redmond Technology Press and has been a contributing editor to a series of bestselling books.

304 pages, paperback, $24.95   Available at bookstores everywhere and at all online bookstores
ISBN: 0-9672981-1-3

DO YOU WANT TO GET A DREAMWEAVER WEB SITE UP AND RUNNING QUICKLY?

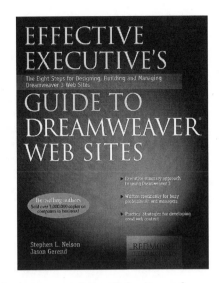

Written specifically for busy executives, managers, and other professionals, *Effective Executive's Guide to Dreamweaver Web Sites* walks you through the eight steps of designing, building, and managing Dreamweaver 3 Web sites:

Step 1: Learn the Logic. Start here with a discussion about how the Web works, why Web sites make sense, and what makes a site effective.

Step 2: Develop a Content Strategy. Identify the purpose of the Web site and the required content.

Step 3: Lay a Foundation. Prepare the foundation of your Web site by getting a domain name and locating a company to host your Web site.

Step 4: Collect and Organize Your Content. Collect existing content or develop new content—then create a central warehouse to store and organize this material.

Step 5: Create Your Web Site. Set up your Web pages and other Web site components using Dreamweaver.

Step 6: Polish Your Pages. Refine your Web pages to make them more effective and professional.

Step 7: Add Interactivity to Your Web Site. Enhance your Web site through the addition of interactive features.

Step 8: Deploy Your Web Site. Test and publish your Web site and then draw attention to it by submitting your site to search engines, sharing links, using newsgroups and list servers, and generating offline publicity.

More than just a book about Dreamweaver, *Effective Executive's Guide to Dreamweaver Web Sites* explains how to create business and nonprofit organization Web sites that really work.

ABOUT THE AUTHORS:

Stephen L. Nelson: With more than 3 million books sold in English, Nelson is arguably the best-selling author writing about using computers in business. Formerly a senior consultant with Arthur Andersen & Co., he is also the co-author of *Effective Executive's Guide to Project 2000* (Redmond Technology Press 2000).

Jason Gerend: Gerend, a freelance technical writer, has contributed to or co-authored a series of acclaimed and best-selling computer books, including *Effective Executive's Guide to FrontPage Web Sites* (Redmond Technology Press 2000).

304 pages, paperback, $24.95   Available at bookstores everywhere and at all online bookstores
ISBN: 0-9672981-9-9

DO YOU WANT TO GET A FRONTPAGE WEB SITE UP AND RUNNING QUICKLY?

Written specifically for busy executives, managers, and other professionals, *Effective Executive's Guide to FrontPage Web Sites* walks you through the eight steps of designing, building, and managing Microsoft FrontPage 2000 Web sites:

Step 1: Learn the Logic. Start here with a discussion about how the Web works, why Web sites make sense, and what makes a site effective.

Step 2: Develop a Content Strategy. Identify the purpose of the Web site and the required content.

Step 3: Lay a Foundation. Prepare the foundation of your Web site by getting a domain name and locating a company to host your Web site.

Step 4: Collect and Organize Your Content. Collect existing content or develop new content—then create a central warehouse to store and organize this material.

Step 5: Create Your Web Site. Set up your Web pages and other Web site components using FrontPage.

Step 6: Polish Your Pages. Refine your Web pages to make them more effective and professional.

Step 7: Add Interactivity to Your Web Site. Enhance your Web site through the addition of interactive features.

Step 8: Deploy Your Web Site. Test and publish your Web site and then draw attention to it by submitting your site to search engines, sharing links, using newsgroups and list servers, and generating offline publicity.

More than just a book about FrontPage, *Effective Executive's Guide to FrontPage Web Sites* explains how to create business and nonprofit organization Web sites that really work.

ABOUT THE AUTHORS:

Stephen L. Nelson: With more than 3 million books sold in English, Nelson is arguably the best-selling author writing about using computers in business. Formerly a senior consultant with Arthur Andersen & Co., he is also the co-author of *Effective Executive's Guide to Project 2000* (Redmond Technology Press 2000).

Jason Gerend: Gerend, a freelance technical writer, has contributed to or co-authored a series of acclaimed and best-selling computer books, including *Effective Executive's Guide to Dreamweaver Web Sites* (Redmond Technology Press 2000).

304 pages, paperback, $24.95   Available at bookstores everywhere and at all online bookstores
ISBN: 0-9672981-3-X